Becoming a Glorious Daughter of the King

Psalm 45:13

Debra L Sommerdorf

Dedication page

This book is dedicated to my daughters Kimberly, Karen, Robin, Shondra and my daughter-in-law LauraLynne. I am grateful for the Lord gifting them to me.

I have tried to give credit on all material that is not mine, that was used to illustrate and illuminate the content of this book to the reader.

To order additional copies, call Debra at 512/626-5373

Becoming a Glorious Daughter of the King
Copyright © 2019 Debra L Sommerdorf

All rights reserved. No part of this book may be reproduced or transmitted in any form or by any means without written permission from the author.

ISBN 978-1-64570-969-5

Printed in USA by 48HrBooks (www.48HrBooks.com)

Table of Contents

Acknowledgement 5
Forward 1 6
Forward 2 7
Introduction 8
Getting Started 9
Part I: *Glorious Within Her Heart* 15
Chapter 1   A Spiritual Heart 16
Chapter 2   A Surrendered Heart 20
Chapter 3   A Strengthened Heart, Putting On 30
Chapter 4   A Strengthened Heart, Filled With 39
After-Action Report 48

Part II: *Glorious Towards Her Husband* 55
Chapter 5   Husbands 57
Chapter 6   Our Goal, Happiness 63
Chapter 7   Love's Goal, Sacrifice 68
Chapter 8   Yielding to Love's Goal 75
After-Action Report 84

Part III: *Glorious Towards Her Heritage* 87
Chapter 9   Heritage 89
Chapter 10   Our First Purpose, Organization 94
Chapter 11   Our Second Purpose, Flexibility 104
Chapter 12   Our Third Purpose, Creativity 113
After-Action Report 118

Part IV: *Glorious In Her Habits* 122
Chapter 13   Glorious in Her Habits 123
Chapter 14   Our Private Habits of Negative Thinking ... 130
Chapter 15   Our Private Habits of Positive Thinking 136
Chapter 16   Glorious in Her Public Habits 142
After-Action Report... 150

Farewell Letter

About the Author

Acknowledgements

I am very grateful for the many prayers and encouraging words from many during my time writing this book. I am especially thankful for my husband who was my sounding board, editor and constant assistant, whether Bible information or computer aid. Thank you to my youngest daughter Shondra, and her gift for drawing which added a wonderful dimension to each chapter. A very big thank you to Karen, my second daughter and busy mom of 3, who was sweet to do all the computer graphics and cover, which were totally out of my league. I also want to thank my family for providing the many illustrations and experiences that added to my life and the writing of this book.

Foreword

I called her 'Momma'... just to myself, that is. She was my very own Titus 2 Momma. I met Debra Sommerdorf when I was newly married and only twenty-two years old. But as I watched her every move during our first lunch together, I knew that someday I wanted to be this kind of wife and mother. Somehow that day, Brother and Mrs. Sommerdorf, their six children, and my husband and I managed to fit into our 'Palace' (a thirty-foot fifth wheel), where I served them roast beef and potatoes. While the six children ate quietly and washed my dishes, I was able to ask Miss Debra many questions regarding marriage and child-rearing. Now, sixteen years later, I am still serving alongside my husband in ministry while homeschooling my six children. Miss Debra, my friend, and mentor is still a Titus 2 Momma in my life.

Since Bro. Sommerdorf is a traveling evangelist, I would only get to see her once every two years when their family would come to speak at our church. Yet, beside her own busy schedule, she always seemed to find time to call me or answer my phone calls. Those phone calls (between personal visits) continued to encourage me to become a loving wife and mother. I began to realize that the life of this quiet but wise woman spoke more about her than her own lips. Some people talk about their big dreams and boast about how they live, but others like Miss Debra just live it!

My dear reader, Miss Debra may not be just a phone call away for you as she has been for me, but she is only a few pages away from sharing her heart, her wisdom, and her practical tips for daily life. After years of seeking the Lord through reading and living the word, Miss Debra puts her wise words on paper to pass on to those who want to hear practical biblical truths that work. She is a quiet woman whose interactions with her children and grandchildren demonstrate discipline, diligence, and love for God. No matter your age, if you have a tender heart which seeks to grow, I guarantee that the Holy Spirit will use 'Becoming a Glorious Daughter of the King' to encourage and propel you forward spiritually. Within these pages you, as the reader, will find not only wisdom from the word of God but also thought-provoking questions that will cause you to search your heart. Miss Debra reaches out to you through this book to encourage you to become a glorious daughter of the King. If you will but open your heart to her words based on God's word, my Titus 2 Momma will impact your life, just as she has impacted mine.

Bethany Davidson

Forward

Dear reader: It is with great enthusiasm that I recommend this book to you. Having had the privilege to be married to Deb for over 35 years, I know the practical wisdom and encouragement that you will receive from her as you journey through this book. Deb has been the steady hand upon the hearts and lives of our children, and without her influence in our home, they would not have the character or be the godly adults that they are today.

I trust that you will enjoy your time together with her as much as I have.

Evangelist David Sommerdorf

Introduction

My husband and I have received many blessings through the years discipling people at our dining room table. A specific topic is chosen and viewed through the scriptures. Questions and practical application with examples help the student to be able to use the material studied. We have found that memorization, open discussion, and a question of the week are a great challenge and help everyone to think and work on the topic until our next study.

It is my desire for this book to be used as a tool in discipleship whether it is used in a group or one on one, once a month or weekly. I have included memory verses that correlate with each lesson and very challenging questions, that can help pinpoint areas that need a little help. Understanding the many abilities and variables in each of our lives I have tried not to tell you what to do but allow you to analyze and determine the steps you need to take to make the changes God has pointed out during our time together. These changes will need lots of prayer if they are going to pass the test of time and become of any eternal value.

Our topic, 'Becoming a Glorious Daughter of the King', has been developed for married women. (Part One and Four can be used for singles or teens.) Our complex life, full of meeting the needs of others, can become rather demanding. We want to be able to serve them to the best of our abilities without sacrificing our walk with the Lord, our testimony, or our spiritual growth. God bless you as you grow in the Lord and strive to be a 'Glorious Daughter of the King'.

...Your Sister in Christ,

Debra Sommerdorf

Getting Started

The idea of pretending and make believe was never more alive than when we were children. We created the world as we imagined it... school, playing house, forts, and kings and queens. When dressing up, cardboard boxes and blankets were instant props. There was no end to the many scenarios we played out. But as we got older, we started to get a taste of the work it would take to make those dreams come true.

Psalm 45:13 says, "The King's Daughter is all Glorious within."

This is not a make-believe idea, but a goal for each of us as ladies, who claim to be born again. It applies to every age and description. Each having our own struggles and set of experiences to work through. Not to mention, the stage of life we are in.

God has a desire for each of his daughters. The habits and character qualities will be the same. Fashioned by the many circumstances a loving Father's hand allows to penetrate the pretend life we are trying to make here on earth. The instruction book, the Bible we carry with us, is always available if we choose to seek out what the Father has for us. Not to mention our daily devotional time, the preaching we receive, Sunday school classes, and the many Spirit filled help books out there.

The word 'glorious' is not a word used often but it has an incredible meaning that so helps us to understand the end our Father has in mind for us. It means; noble, excellent, very honorable.

Wow! In other words, not a counterfeit.

My husband gave me a beautiful ring recently. It has three larger diamonds in the center surrounded by a row of smaller diamonds on either side. I love the way it sparkles and catches the light. It is very precious to me and I am very careful when I wear it. There are times when I am doing chores or being messy, that I put another ring on. It is also very pretty. It has one nice size stone and several little ones on one side of the band. It is very striking, but it is not real. I paid 29 dollars for it. It is just a piece of costume jewelry. The stones are cubic zirconium, nothing special. It has a purpose, but the other ring has real value.

If you and I were given the opportunity to choose, we would not hesitate to pick the real one.

Our heavenly Father is also looking for what is real and valuable. It is easy for him to spot a counterfeit, and it grieves his heart. He has the ability to cut away at our religious façade, hidden sin and pious attitudes. He sees us for who we really are and knows the motivation of our actions. Would He be able to pick you as one of his 'glorious' daughters?

A good Bible definition would be:

> *Colossians 1:10...That ye might walk worthy of the Lord unto all pleasing, being fruitful in every good work, and increasing in the knowledge of God.*

This verse has great depth for a daily walk of growth for a Christian. If we are not careful to take the time to dig a little, we could miss an incredible truth. Let's go back and reread it.

That ye- makes it very personal. Despite whatever anyone else is doing. It also has the idea that you are responsible for the growth in your own Christian walk.

might walk- walking has the idea of progression, taking action one step at a time, maybe not fast, but always moving in a direction.

worthy of the Lord- having value. Honorable, admirable or deserving of recognition from the Lord's perspective.

unto all pleasing- another way of looking at this, is to think that the actions and ideas of my life would put a smile on my Father's face. He is the one we are trying to please.

being fruitful- producing a return, results take time.

During my many years in Alaska I have planted many gardens. Lots of work was involved in getting it to produce the desired vegetables. One thing I noticed was no matter how perfect the conditions were, some fruit took more time to mature than others.

This is the same with character qualities of spiritual fruit. Our personalities and experiences make it easier for some fruit to grow, while others seem to be impossible. But don't give up! Keep weeding, watering, and fertilizing. There is a bumper crop of character to harvest if you are willing to work for it.

good work- a task to do that takes energy. It is defined as a 'good' work. Unfortunately, we must define good. This is not what we label good, or what society tells us is good, but what the Bible describes as good. God is so clear in his word on what is pleasing and what is just flat out wrong!

Work! The one thing we try to avoid at all cost. Yes, this idea of becoming 'glorious' is going to require some sweat and tears. It is not for the weak and faint hearted, but the rewards are so worth it! Not just for us, but for the many we meet and influence every day.

increasing- growing and progressing. Not staying the same but allowing the power of the Lord to work in us and through us.

in the knowledge of God- God was so wise in giving us a never changing, yet always current manual on how to live our Christian life. There are many opinions out there, but we need to go to God's Word and put His desires into practice in our lives.

Becoming **'glorious'** can be a daunting task.

While living in Alaska we would often visit a place called the 'Butte'. It was a beautiful out cropping of a hill in the middle of a valley. There were many great views on the way up, but at the top it would take your breath away. A 360-degree panoramic scene overlooking the Matanuska Valley, the Knick Glacier and the majestic Chugiak Mountain Range. (Pioneer Peak being the most prominent). It is one of those places you can jump in the air, have someone take a picture, and look like you are falling with glaciers and snow-covered mountains behind you.

Getting there was a great undertaking, though. Almost 1,000 feet to the summit, and 900 steps and pull ropes to assist when the trail became too steep, the 2-mile path always seemed to keep ascending upward.

As we begin our journey towards becoming that '**glorious**' daughter in Psalm 45:13, I think the first step would be to ask our Heavenly Father to guide and help us along the way.

Dear Heavenly Father,

Thank you for your great love for me. Looking at my life I see a great need to grow closer to you and accomplish the many specific tasks you have created me for. I have wasted precious time doing my own thing. Please forgive me. I find myself needing your strength to be more like that glorious daughter that I find in your word. Many times, I do not have the ability to make the changes that I need or to be faithful long term to see the fruit I know you have for me to bear. My greatest desire is to bring you glory. Please help me accomplish this in my life.

In Jesus name, Amen.

A little Homework...

A. *By your actions who is the one you are ultimately trying to please? (You will need to be truthful with yourself if you want to see growth in your life.)*

        Parents, Friends, Church, Society
        Your dreams, Yourself, the Lord, others...

B. *How would you grade your position as a daughter of the King?*
   1. disobedient and rebellious
   2. distant and struggling to commit.
   3. obedient, but not intimate
   4. growing and moving closer
   5. loving and faithful, the apple of His eye

C. *What would be some of the benefits of becoming that* ***'glorious'*** *daughter?*
   1.
   2.
   3.

D. *Are you willing to roll up your sleeves and go to work to become a* ***'glorious'*** *daughter?*

E. *Who would be a lady you know that you consider to be a* ***'glorious'*** *daughter?*

F. *What are a couple of habits she has that you could implement in your life?*
   1.
   2.
   3.

G. *Make a plan to put these habits into your life.*
   1.
   2.
   3.
   4.

H. *Spend some time with this 'glorious' daughter on a regular basis. Ask some questions, but also do lots of listening. After each time together write down what she said or did, as well as what she didn't say or do. There is more to be learned by observing and then doing. Volunteer to assist her in a ministry.*

I. *In prayer twice a day ask the Lord to:*

    1.
    2.
    3.
    4.

J. *What is the definition of glorious?*

K. *List 2 activities or attitudes that are not good in your life and list a two-step plan to make them* **good** *and* ***fruitful*** *before the Lord?*

Memory verse

Colossians 1:10...*That ye might walk worthy of the Lord unto all pleasing, being fruitful in every good work, and increasing in the knowledge of God.*

Part One

Glorious Within Her Heart

Chapter One

A Spiritual Heart

We know that not all daughters are glorious all the time. They, like we, are prone to make selfish decisions, be disobedient and many times, just not do what they are supposed to do. That doesn't mean they change families. But they are not in favor with the rest of the members.

I have been blessed with 6 children of which 4 are daughters. There have been many days while they were young, that one or more of them were not on my favorite list. Their disobedience created a breach in our relationship. I will admit, I wanted to disown them at times, but could not. I remember one occasion when I was on the phone with a lady from church, (back in the day when the phone was tied to the receiver), I was multitasking and emptying the dishwasher. By chance, I picked up my china gravy bowl and as I raised to put it in the cupboard, I notice a crooked crack running all the way across the base. It had been secretly glued together and placed in the dishwasher. I immediately called for my daughter, Karen, knowing that she would be the only one that creative and sneaky to come up with such a plan. I was not happy with her at all! But it did not remove her from being my daughter. (Just recently I gifted that bowl to her as a reminder of the mercy extended to her).

The Big question is…**Where should we be 'Glorious'?**

The first place we need to be 'Glorious' is Within our Hearts!

This speaks of her relationship with her spiritual King. Her Heavenly Father. But we have one big problem. We don't begin with a Glorious Heart.

> **Jeremiah 17:9…** *The heart is deceitful above all things, and desperately wicked: who can know it?*

The idea that we are basically good, and when put in the right atmosphere will make the right choices, is a great myth. Our heart is always looking out for self.

Early in our ministry a homeless man came to our door asking for some money. My husband offered to take him and feed him, looking for an opportunity to share the gospel and the love of Christ with him. He picked up some medications and a few clothing items for him, then took him to get a background report printed out so he could spend a few nights in a halfway house. While waiting at the police station, the man went out to smoke a cigarette. The officer behind the counter requested my husband to come into the office. As soon as he entered, she slammed the door shut and asked, "How long have you known this guy?" Confused my husband replied, "A few hours, why?" "Do you know that he is wanted in five states?" she responded. Well, that was not the story he told my husband. He very convincingly shared a completely different story. He shared his story so earnestly that my husband had no reason to doubt him. You see, in his desperation he had learned to become incredibly deceitful.

Our heart tells us that we are OK. We don't really feel like we deserve hell or any serious consequence at all. In fact, we believe that since we have never been put behind bars or participated in one of the "unpardonable" sins, we are OK. There are so many people much worse than us. We have this idea that God will understand. This sounds so insignificant, but it is not!

Romans 3:10-12...*As it is written, There is none righteous, no, not one: there is none that doeth good, no, not one.*

Thankfully, God seeing this great need, planned a three-step solution to deal with our hearts.

Our first step is recognizing our need for a Spiritual Heart.

> *John 3:16...For God so loved the world, that he gave his only begotten Son, that whosoever believeth in him should not perish, but have everlasting life.*

I cannot find a better verse that so sums up God's love for us. It's the one verse in the Bible practically everyone knows. What sacrifice to give your only son to be tortured and hung on a cross. For what? Nothing more than to rescue self-willed, sinful man. And what was he asking in return? For us to believe in the only one who could forgive our sins, making them white as snow.

I was blessed to be raised in a Christian home. At the age of seven I accepted the Lord in my heart during a 'Good News Club' held in our home every week. During that time, I started applying the Bible stories that I had heard for years to myself and saw my need for salvation. The lady who led the club, Mrs. Carothers, used the familiar Bible stories to show me my need for forgiveness.

A little Homework...

One of our favorite things to do when meeting new people is to hear where and how they got saved. It is very exciting to hear what God has done in someone else's life and the steps they took to receive him. It also rekindles the fire of your own salvation experience.

1. *Have you ever been saved?*

2. *Take the time to write down your salvation experience. Don't forget what brought you to consider your need to be saved, the people involved, some verses that were used, and what changed right away in your life. (If in a group setting, this would be a great Show-n-Tell for next week.)*

3. Thank the Lord for your salvation.

4. Who were the ones responsible to give you the gospel? You might want to call those instrumental in leading you to the Lord and thank them for investing in your life.

5. Who can you share your salvation testimony with this week?

6. Do you have a Bible reading program? A phone app, <u>Bible.is</u>, is an audio-dramatized reading of God's Word. Great for when you are doing non-mental tasks.

Memory verse

Proverbs 4:23...*Keep thy heart with all diligence; for out of it are the issues of life.*

Glorious Within Her Heart

Chapter Two

A Surrendered Heart

The second step we need to take in this area of our hearts is the Surrendered Heart. It is very important that we don't get these in the wrong order. Many children that have been raised in church find themselves accepting truths that they have heard all their life but have never come to a personally accepting of what Christ has done for them. They conform to a way of living but are many times living with continual doubts. There is a lack of joy, victory over sin and power in their life. Before moving on, Please, make sure you have trusted this wonderful Savior.

> **Psalm 139:23,24**...*Search me, O God, and know my heart: try me, and know my thoughts: And see if there be any wicked way in me, and lead me in the way everlasting.*

What a great verse to start with in this second step, the Surrendered Heart.

The first thing I notice about this verse is that out of all creation God has given man a free will. This means, unlike animals, we choose to have a relationship with him. We can purposely seek out His company. Will we obey his commands, thus receiving the blessings he has in store for us or do we do it our way and hope everything will turn out all right and face eternity without him? Even the term 'father' suggests intimacy and one involved in guiding and controlling areas of another's life.

...Search me, O God, and know my heart,

Gives us the idea that we come to realize that on our own we mess things up and need to give our Heavenly Father permission to show us where we are wrong. We acknowledge that something is wrong that we have caused, and we can't fix it. It could be something done or not done in ignorance. It might be an attitude that we dismiss and has become a habit, or an action. Sometimes it's a way of thinking that nobody else even knows exists. It could be something that we allow because we swallow the lie 'this is the way God made me'. Nonetheless, we need to humble ourselves and allow our Father to do his work in our life with no reservation.

> ***Psalm 40:2**...He brought me up also out of an horrible pit, out of the miry clay, and set my feet upon a rock, and established my goings.*

Many of us try to rely on our own abilities to change ourselves. Can you even begin to count the many times you set a New Year's resolution or turned over a new leaf? These and other well-meaning ideas quickly come to an end and get added to the pile of 'I give up. It's just too hard'. The world and its ideas seem to cling to us like quicksand. We wear out and just end up going back to what our flesh does naturally.

If we are to have any results, we need to get the assistance of someone more powerful than us. And who would be more qualified than our Heavenly Father! He who created us with such care and purpose. He has set an incredible track record in the lives of great people. People like Saul, who tortured and killed Christians until that day on the road to Damascus where the Lord confronted him. After that he wrote 13 books of the New Testament, made three missionary journeys, and became God's chosen vessel to the Gentiles. Or Rahab the harlot, a Gentile, who lived in that wicked city Jericho, and trusted in the God of the Israelites and ended up in the lineage of the Messiah.

Not too long ago our son called and said that our grandson, age four, was tearing around church knocking the little ones off their feet. Kevin stopped him and asked," What are you doing?" to which he replied," I Duperman!" with great gusto and pride. Our son went on to explain that Superman went around doing good. Without hesitation Daniel replied, "I evil Duperman!" What a picture of our heart bent on doing whatever makes it happy.

Surrender would be a good word to describe the attitude we should have. It means to give up or yield. In other words, "To raise the white flag." Now this is not a partial surrender. It is handing over every key to every room of our heart. We have an evangelist friend, Tom Gilliam, who says…'God doesn't want first place in your heart, He wants ALL the places.'

I Peter 5:6…Humble yourselves therefore under the mighty hand of God, that he may exalt you in due time.

The next thing is **confession**. That word itself kind of smarts. It means to admit and tell the truth. None of us enjoys being corrected, let alone having to admit our faults. We become very creative in finding an excuse or blaming someone or something for what we are guilty of. God has given us His Word to define right and wrong and to help us separate the good from the evil. That is why it is so important to have a daily Bible reading program.

Psalm 119:105…Thy word is a lamp unto my feet, and a light unto my path.

One of the excuses I hear rather often is, "I can't help it. God made me that way". What a sad excuse, to blame the one who paid the ultimate price in life by dying on the cross.

　…try me,

Wow! Did I read that right? We are to be in such a close union with the Lord that we ask him to test us. It seems to say, "I have done everything your word has told me to do. I am living, to the best of my ability, to bring you glory. Challenge me Lord, I can do it. Just watch!"

...and know every thought: And see if there be any wicked way in me,

We need to come to the place where we can give the Lord the permission to investigate every thought and deed. Why every thought? "My thoughts aren't hurting anyone, you say." Well, before any action can be done or word spoken, it is a thought. Not that we plan it out in our mind but that the desires of our hearts come out. You never think one thing and do something else. If you find yourself participating in something not pleasing to the Lord or to your liking, check out your heart.

An Indian, who was a new believer, was asked" How are you doing?" He said," I find two dogs fighting within me. A black dog and a white dog". "Which one wins?" he was asked. "The one I feed the most," was his reply.

If we choose to feed our selfish flesh than we will began to shrivel up spiritually. But if we read God's word, spend time in prayer and get under the teaching of His word, our spirit will grow stronger and we have the strength to say no to sin and see fruit in our Spiritual Heart.

Proverbs 23:7...For as he thinketh in his heart, so is he.

Proverbs 16:2...All the ways of a man are clean in his own eyes; but the Lord weigheth the spirits.

….and lead me in the way everlasting.

It's amazing the many choices we have. From choosing cold cereal, type of vehicle to drive, music, exercise styles and so much more. We face choices everywhere we turn. Most of these choices have no lasting consequence, but when you begin to think about your future and the steps to get to a desired end, well that's another story. Decisions on which school, education program, career, marriage partner are just a few of these choices. If we are not careful, we will make them with the limited wisdom and experience we have. Many don't even consider the character qualities you need to be exercising to be able to attain these goals. They think they will just miraculously appear when you need them. What a wake-up call.

> ***Proverbs 3:6***...*In all thy ways acknowledge him, and he shall direct thy paths.*
> ***Proverbs 14:12***...*There is a way which seemeth right unto a man, but the end thereof are the ways of death.*

Part of having a **Surrendered Heart** is the ability to identify things that we need to get out of our life. God made it very clear for us in His word concerning the things that are displeasing and should not be allowed. Colossians 3:5 starts with the word, 'mortify'. It means to put to death or kill. God is very serious about us becoming 'glorious' and eliminating what is displeasing to him. Let's look at a few of these battles.

> ***Colossians 3:8,9***...*But now ye also put off all these; anger, wrath, malice, blasphemy, filthy communication out of your mouth. Lie not one to another, seeing that ye have put off the old man with his deeds.*

The first thing we see is that God starts with a command. Put off! It's not an option! Take it off and never put it on again. There is no exception. God does not want us to have any form of these character traits in his 'glorious' daughters.

Put Off:
    <u>**anger**</u>- no control, jumps right out there, hostile
    <u>**wrath**</u>- simmers and loses it, extreme anger, rage, fury
    <u>**malice**</u>- planning to get even, vengeful, enmity

> ***Proverbs 29:22**...An angry man stirreth up strife, and a furious man aboundeth in transgression.*

In our busy life we have become accustomed to getting what we want and how we want it. We loudly complain if we must wait for our food in the microwave or get stuck in traffic on the expressway. Anything that slows us down creates stress no matter how small it is. When we react to these situations in anger or wrath, we need to realize that we are abounding in transgression and sin.

Many of you have children at home and they can have multiple accidents in a day. Because they are in training you are constantly correcting them. This can be very exhausting. We need to guard against losing control. Our goal is to train them to be in control and it does us no good if we are out of control when we are training them.

blasphemy- to mock or destroy one's character, tear down (in word or deed)

At first glance you would say I am safe from this one. I do not take the Lord's name in vain. If that were the only meaning this word has, you would probably be right. We need to look at the rest of the definition that is often overlooked.

It's amazing to me the many people who use someone else as an excuse not to listen to the gospel or even consider going to church. It's not uncommon to hear someone share how their parents were one thing at home and another at church. They had the feeling that church was more important than them. Singing in the choir, teaching Sunday school, church secretary, but at home...well, I leave that to you. Children are always watching and weighing things out. They see a mom who is angry at home, arguing or not obeying dad and just too busy to give them a little time and love. They are required to behave in a godly manner with strong consequences but see very little self-discipline on the parent's part.

Some have had business dealings with Christians. They have found them to be untrustworthy even to the point of not paying their bills. Here is an illustration I read.

A pastor made a visit to a dentist who had been visiting church for several weeks. Though unsaved, he would never come forward at the invitation. Upon inquiring as to why he wouldn't respond, the dentist said," I know I need to be saved but when I see several of your people in the choir singing through teeth they have never paid for, I doubt this God who you say can change lives."

> ***II Samuel 12:14...Howbeit, by this deed thou hast given great occasion to the enemies of the LORD to blaspheme...***
> *(David's sin with Bathsheba and Uriah)*

Could it be that we are living in such a way that we blaspheme the name of the Lord? How are you viewed by those around you? A counterfeit? Or in time to come would you hear that because of your example someone chose to follow the Lord. It could be a coworker, family member, church member, spouse, or child. What a heavy responsibility, but what reason for rejoicing to hear you made a difference in a life.

filthy communication out of your mouth:

I love the illustration about our tongues being put behind the prison bars of our teeth. Unfortunately, we allow too much to slip past them.

1. lies or twisting the truth. Colossians 3:9...Lie not one to another, seeing that ye have put off the old man with his deeds.

2. gossip: sharing with the purpose of lifting one's self up or tearing down one another, language that is usually directed against an individual.

3. Sarcasm: a sharp or caustic utterance designed to cause pain.

> ***James 3:6...****And the tongue is a fire, a world of iniquity: so is the tongue among our members, that it defileth the whole body, and setteth on fire the course of nature; and it is set on fire of Hell.*
> ***Titus 3:2*** *Speak evil of no man...*

Wow! What a thought. Very little explanation is needed here. I just want to say that 'no man', means no one without exception. Position, wealth, talents, or any other category is not mentioned.

This, in no way is an exhaustive list of the things we need to 'put off' in our lives. But it is a start. As you grow in the Lord, he will show you other habits that are not becoming to one of his 'glorious daughters.'

That was a pretty big step. We are going to need to invest time and energy for this to happen in our lives. God is looking for the Surrendered Heart. He has an incredible plan for your life and is just waiting for you to take that next step.

A little Homework...

    A. *How would you describe your time in the Word of God?*
    1. nonexistent
    2. only at church
    3. in time of need
    4. somewhat faithfully
    5. constantly every day

B. How would you describe your personal prayer life?
 1. nonexistent
 2. during meals only
 3. meals and church
 4. regimentally scheduled
 5. constant and very vibrant

C. What is one habit that needs to change in your life?

  1. What consequence or damage has occurred because of this habit?

  2. List two steps that you can take to change this habit into a God-honoring habit?

D. Find a Bible reading schedule and begin a daily time of reading and praying.

E. Make a point this week to not allow any, "filthy communication out of your mouth."

F. Are you holding back a key to a room of your heart? What would it be? and why?

G. Write the words that fit in these categories that you used this last week.

angry words-

lies-

gossip-

sarcasm-

H. Can you say to the Lord right now, try me? If not, what area has you concerned?

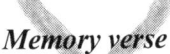

Memory verse

Psalms 139:23,24...*Search me, O God, and know my heart: try me, and know my thoughts: And see if there be any wicked way in me, and lead me in the way everlasting.*

Glorious Within Her Heart

Chapter Three

The Strengthened Heart: putting on

We are ready for the third step in this 'glorious' heart. Now that we have cleared some of the debris from our life, it is time to build. Just like our physical body needs several things to help it grow properly, our spiritual body does also. God does not want us to stay in the condition he found us. It's also good to know that just like children we grow at different stages and in different areas. The image of the Lord is our goal.

> *II Peter 3:18...But grow in grace, and in the knowledge of our Lord and Saviour Jesus Christ. To him be glory both now and forever. Amen.*

In the previous chapter we talked about some of the things He wants us to 'put off'. How are you doing with that? Keep putting off. It's a continual practice. In the long run you will reap so many benefits.

Today we are going to do some building and 'Putting On'.

Again, as 'putting off' was a command, so is this idea of 'putting on'. We need to be filling the space that is now emptied from the many things we have taken off. Something will fill the emptiness that is left, and God wants it to be God honoring habits that are spoken about in His word. These new attitudes and habits are not natural to our flesh. We tend to operate with the idea with what is best for me. As we grow, we begin to ask the question what would the Lord have me to do? Let's look at a few and see what they have to offer.

> *Colossians 3:10, 12-15...And have put on the new man, which is renewed in knowledge after the image of him that created him: Put on therefore, as the elect of God, holy and beloved, bowels of mercies, kindness, humbleness of mind, meekness, longsuffering; Forbearing one another and forgiving one another, if any man have a quarrel against any: even as Christ forgave you, so also do ye. And above all these things put on charity, which is the bond of perfectness. And let the peace of God rule in your hearts, to the which also ye are called in one body; and be ye thankful.*

holy- dedicated to God or sacred
This has the idea of searching and confessing sin while becoming faithful to living a life pleasing to the Lord. We ask the question, "Is what I'm about to do or think, bring a smile on my heavenly Father's face?" We live to please Him.

mercy- undeserved kindness (it uses the term, 'bowels of', which means, 'comes from your inner being or roots'. It's a constant habit)

kindness- preferring others above yourself, meeting a need.
In our Christian life we tend to operate like the blind man that saw men as trees in Mark 8:24. We are so focused on 'our 4 and no more' or the rut of going and doing our normal Christian business that we don't see the need that is walking or sitting beside us. People were always the Lord's focus and he above all of us had lots to do. Do you see the needs and hurt around you? Are you trying to help and meet some of those needs?

humbleness of mind- not proud or boastful.

During the time of the New Testament there were a group of people known as the Pharisees. They were big on public prayer and proclaiming the many deeds they did. Quick to point out faults in others and careful not to be outdone by any. They have been associated with whited sepulchers, meaning clean on the outside but full of dead men's bones on the inside...Matthew 23:27. We need to make sure that everything we do is for the Lord, and if no one sees it we still would be caught doing it because it is right.

meekness- restraining one's own power, humble, teachable.

> *Galatians 6:1...Brethren, if a man be overtaken in a fault, ye which are spiritual restore such an one in the spirit of meekness; considering thyself, lest thou also be tempted.*

The words, 'ye which are spiritual restore such an one' are often ignored. We see something out of line or wrong and we are going to set it right in whatever spirit we are in. But our goal, if we are walking with the Lord, is to be able to point out wrong without destroying the desire to continue in the right direction. That takes lots of wisdom and kindness. We forget that without the grace of God, 'there go I'. Let's remember to build and be thankful for God's forgiveness and patience.

One of the challenging times for a parent is when the children begin to practice driving. On one of those days when my oldest son and I were the only ones in the car, I began to remind him of the need to slow down, especially coming up on turns or stop signs. He assured me life was good and I had no need to worry. 'Driving is easy, you know.' Thankfully, traffic in this area of Alaska was sparse. He proceeded to put his right arm on the back of the seat and his left dropped to the bottom of the steering wheel. Relaxing in a, 'I have everything under control attitude'. He made the last turn before our street and asked very confidently, "How did I do?" I complimented him on his speed before intersections, use of turning signals and mirrors, and his watchful eye for traffic and how he had done a great job! My only concern was that we were now driving in oncoming traffic. Immediately he sat up straight and positioned his hands on three and nine o'clock and moved the car into the proper lane. Nothing more needed to be said. The reality that he needed more practice was accepted. Until I started teaching this lesson this story was kept a secret. You see, Kevin has four sisters, and I didn't want to embarrass him.

> *II Timothy 2:25...In meekness instructing those that oppose themselves...*

longsuffering- suffering long or patient, the ability to stay calm. (we will study this a little more in the next lesson)

forbearing- behaving or restraint in relationships.

Today we are bombarded in a society that places no restrictions on anything. Whatever makes you happy is OK. Respect for others or their things is hardly a thought. But God's word is very specific in our treatment of others. People belong to God. He created them individually with a specific purpose in mind. We have no right to treat them any way we like. Timothy says we are to treat every relationship 'with all purity'. That means not getting them flawed or dirty in any way. Spouse, children, elderly, or peers.

As women we must take into consideration the men that are around us and not act or dress in such a way as to incite lust in their hearts. Teasing can be fun in a mixed crowd, but we must be careful that it doesn't lead to flirting. Men are aroused by sight. Thus, we need to choose attire that is attractive but not revealing. I love the saying, 'Dress in such a way that men know that you are a woman, but that they also know you are a lady.'

> *I Timothy 3:15...That thou mayest know how thou oughtest to behave thyself in the house of God.*
> *I Timothy 5:1,2...Rebuke not an elder, but intreat him as a father; and the younger men as brethren; The elder women as mothers; the younger as sisters, with all purity.*

forgiving- letting something go even before asked.

    When I read stories about World War II and the Holocaust, I wonder how any human could do such atrocities to an innocent person and feel justified in doing so. I look at those who have been mistreated and think that if anyone has a right to be bitter, these people have that right. Corrie ten Boom shares a story in one of her books where, following the war, she meets one of the guards from her prison camp. He was very cruel, and many died at his hand. When they met, he held out his hand and said, "Corrie, God has forgiven me, now I am asking you to forgive me, as well." Time stood still as she remembered her sister's death and many of the horrors at the hands of the guards. God spoke to her and said if she could not forgive this man, her ministry would be over. She slowly forced herself to raise her hand to meet his and prayed," God, could you forgive this man through me?" The moment their hands touched, God's love and forgiveness flowed through her and she was able to say in her heart, "I forgive you." Could it be we need to make the first move before we feel the wounds and breaches begin to heal?

    I love the story in Luke 7:36-50 where Jesus eats at Simon's house and a woman comes and anoints the Lords feet and washes them with her hair. He tells Simon a parable and then said, *"Wherefore I say unto thee, her sins, which are many, are forgiven: for she loved much: but to whom little is forgiven the same loveth little."* How much of your sin is forgiven? If we could just remember what we have been forgiven, we would be more tolerant of others.

charity- love in action, works of unselfishness.

Christianity today tries to make charity all about love and feelings. The Lord only proved his love in the actions he did. He wasn't looking to spread love or happiness but to meet our true heart's need. A good way to remember charity is love with work gloves on. Putting what you know to work helping those around you. Unselfishly giving and sacrificing to meet the needs of others.

peace- trusting God with whatever comes in my life.

Have you noticed all the unseen things that you didn't plan on? We try so hard to control our and other's circumstances. But to no avail. Many people are suffering from stress disorders and looking for magical relief but never giving up and accepting the situation as it is. The idea, 'I can only find true happiness when life is what I deem it to be', leads only to misery. This does not mean we roll over and play dead. We need to add a little contentment to our life and then look for the things we can change for the betterment of everyone involved. Why did I add that last part? I have noticed that we are often willing to get what we want at the expense of our children, husband or our relationship with God. But this is for another study.

How do I cope with this financial need? What about this medical situation? My child is chasing the world, or my husband has had an affair. These are some major events that you will need to go to your pastor for counsel and help. Will one dose of peace bring about trust that doesn't doubt or worry? No. Sometimes it is a moment-by-moment application. God is faithful to be there with you as you go through your storm.

> ***II Corinthians 12:9***...*My grace is sufficient for thee: for my strength is made perfect in weakness. Most gladly therefore will I rather glory in my infirmities, that the power of Christ may rest upon me.*
> ***I Timothy 6:6***...*But godliness with contentment is great gain. For we brought nothing into this world, and it is certain we can carry nothing out. And having food and raiment let us be therewith content.*

<u>thankful</u>- feeling or expressing gratitude, appreciative.

Thank you! It's not difficult to say, but you will find it hardly used. We take so much for granted. Selfishness and complaining are a habit in so many lives. Luke 17 tells the story of 10 lepers being healed, but only one came back to say, "Thank you!" I can't imagine such a horrible disease to live and die with. Yet, here are men that have lived with the reality of no hope. They find the Savior, and he heals them for free. Not partially, but all at once and completely. What things in your life do you take for granted? Would you like to be grouped with the nine or the one?

> ***Ephesians 5:20***...*Giving thanks always for all things unto God and the Father.*

Wow! What a list! You ask, "what happened with going to church, singing in the choir and not drinking?" Well, God knows that if we put this new man on, those other outward things will naturally appear. Our outer man and actions are a picture of the heart. This is why God is so interested in our hearts being governed by His word. He is looking for the 'glorious heart' and he is sure to find all of these traits in daily practice there.

A little Homework...

A. *Are you current with your daily Bible reading?*

B. *Search out someone obscure and meet a need in their life. How or what would Jesus do for them if he were there?*

C. *Write down 2 habits that you are involved in that are performance based. The ones the Lord would say are stealing the glory from Him while neglecting a God given responsibility.*

D. *Look back and see if there is a situation that you handled poorly. Write it down. Pray the Lord would forgive you and go to that one and make it right. Remember it's not who's right but what's right.*

E. *Is there something in your life that you are having trouble letting go of and forgiving? Take the time to write it down in detail and ask the Lord daily to help you forgive that person and/or event.*

F. See if you can come up with a list of 100 things you are thankful for. Look for opportunities to say thank you this week.

G. Could you be causing another man to sin with your attire or conversation? Guard your time with the opposite sex. Don't allow the devil to use you to be a stumbling block to others.

H. Without looking back, see if you can list the nine things we are supposed to 'put on' and a brief definition.

1.

2.

3.

4.

5.

6.

7.

8.

9.

Memory verse

II Peter 3:18...But grow in grace, and in the knowledge of our Lord and Saviour Jesus Christ. To him be glory both now and forever. Amen!

Glorious Within Her Heart

Chapter Four

The Strengthened Heart:
filled with

There is another group of verses that we need to investigate. We often refer to them as the 'Fruit of the Spirit'. You will notice that some of them will be repeated from our study last time in the book of Colossians.

> *Galatians 5:22,23...But the fruit of the Spirit is love, joy, peace, longsuffering, gentleness, goodness, faith, Meekness, temperance: against such there is no law.*

Fruit is something we must nurture and feed. It doesn't just show up in your life. You will have to make a conscious effort for it to become a natural byproduct in your life. Some are easier for different personalities and when it's the most important time to use them, it will also be the most difficult time.

<u>love</u>: sacrifice, act of the will not emotions.

Life is very messy and noisy if you are a mom. Young children go about their day making and creating work and are unable to see the disaster they leave in their wake. Because of our love for our children we continue picking up after them and meeting their needs. The diapers get changed and the midnight feedings become our routine. This is a great picture of true love.

It isn't because they deserve it or will repay us, but because we love them.

Marriage is another way we practice the love of God. It isn't long after the wedding that we come to a place that we exercise the love our spouse needs. They forget an important date, we need help, but they are oblivious and don't get involved. Or the big one...we send them female vibes, but they have no way of deciphering them. Have you been there? Despite the daily circumstances of life, and the things that appear that we were to blind to when we were dating, we come to a decision. Do we choose to love from the heart because it is right in the sight of God, or do we harp and exist in an unhappy marriage?

joy- true joy does not depend on your circumstances.

I enjoy listening to Christian radio and one day Joni Eareckson Tada was speaking. (She is a quadriplegic.) She was sharing how a lady asked her about the joy that she felt whenever she was around her. Joni began to explain that when her husband leaves for work that she has one hour alone in bed until a friend comes to help her get ready for the day. During that time, she pleads with God to take her life and set her free from this prison of her body. She is tired of being helpless and sitting all day in her chair waiting for others to take care of her every need. She ends her hour asking the Lord, that if he can get any glory out of her life, she surrenders it to him. That is true joy.

Has life taken your joy away and you find yourself spending most of the time under a rain cloud? It's time to come out into the sunshine. There's a deeper joy that only comes from Him. Ask Him to become very real to you, to fill you with His joy, to get glory out of your life, and allow you to be a blessing to others.

Psalm, 16:11...In thy presence is fullness of joy.

peace- trusting God with whatever comes in your life.

God knows and allows the circumstances that we face. Sometimes it is the consequences of our choices. We do reap what we sow. When you get pulled over for speeding, it isn't God's fault. At other times he brings things in our lives for us to grow and learn to draw on His grace. Someone said, 'it's not the absence of conflict, but the presence of God that brings peace'.

Billie was a friend of mine and at 21 she was diagnosed with MS. During the many years that she fought this disease, she served God and raised four children. Her favorite saying was, 'God is good all the time!'. She trusted her Lord in every circumstance of her life, not complaining. At her funeral one of her sons spoke and said that if mom had blamed God and gotten bitter, he doubted that any of them would be serving the Lord. She found a peace in trusting her God. Are you on the brink of bitterness? Look to the Lord and find that peace that passes all understanding.

Philippians 4:7...And the peace of God, which passeth all understanding, shall keep your hearts and minds through Christ Jesus.
Proverbs 16:32a...He that is slow to anger is better than the mighty.

longsuffering- patient, suffers long.

Patience is one of the hardest things to exercise. We don't have time for accidents or waiting. It's the opposite of anger, wrath, and malice. We learned about them in chapter three. But life is full of things that slow us down and get in our way. Besides life, have you noticed God doesn't operate in our time frame either? Abraham was promised a son and 10 years later Isaac appears. Years after that God told him to offer Isaac as a sacrifice. I bet Abraham did not see that coming. The miraculous birth was astounding, but he was also promised that through Isaac a nation would be born. Have you ever stumbled with what God is doing in your life? We tend to pray and want an answer, or the need met immediately. We need to wait on the Lord. We need to exercise some longsuffering in our spiritual walk.

gentleness- meek or humble, docile, easy to work with, a submissive spirit.

> ***James 3:17a...**But the wisdom that is from above is first pure, then peaceable, gentle, and easy to be intreated, full of mercy and good fruits, without partiality, and without hypocrisy.*

My granddaughter Noel loves elephants. She calls them Dumbos. They are so big and strong but are led about easily with a rope or chain. Many times, they are tied up to a tent stake. They can easily pull it out of the ground if they wanted to, but they don't. When they were young, they were tied to something very sturdy and strong. They tried repeatedly to get free. Finally, they gave up. Now a simple lead will control them.

The Lord wants us to be like that elephant. Are you easy to work with? Can your family testify that you have a submissive spirit? I think we can all improve in this area.

faith- trusting what you can't see or understand.

> ***Hebrews 11:1...**Now faith is the substance of things hoped for, the evidence of things not seen.*

In I Samuel 1, we learn about a barren woman named Hannah. She was so distraught she refused to eat, and nothing made her happy. (read her story to fill in the details) During a visit to the temple, the high priest promised her a son. After that, the Bible says in verse 18, 'that she went her way, and did eat, and her countenance was no more sad.' She had no immediate change in her body to trust in. She exercised faith. She believed the promise and the word spoken by the priest.

Giving our future and dreams over to someone else and trusting them to decide every detail can be scary. But that is what God wants us to do. Trust Him to make the decisions. This is living by faith. What if it doesn't make me happy? The reality of everything happening the way we want it is impossible! What if God's desire for you or one of your children is the mission field? What if God allows an accident or disease in your life or someone close to you? Just think of the many things God has in store for you along your way that you would miss if you refused to trust him. The day we turn our life over to the Lord we are saying I trust you for whatever you bring in my life and am willing to go anywhere and do anything.

> ***Proverbs 3:5,6**...Trust in the Lord with all thine heart; and lean not unto thine own understanding. In all thy ways acknowledge him, and he shall direct thy paths.*

Many of us have memorized these verses. They speak about us, 'Giving up the Control,' in our lives and allowing the Lord to pick the path we are to take. That is faith. It has several unknowns...
    we don't know where it will lead.
    it's not always easy.
    sometimes it's a cross we must carry.

My husband felt the call to Alaska to help start churches. We married and moved into a 45 ft. trailer in North Pole. It was summer, no problem. But then winter came. We had to put insulation in the windows and thick blankets over them. The frost came in on the screws and any clothing against the wall froze to it. We had to move our baby's crib into the center of the room, so she wouldn't get cold. It stayed 40 below zero for weeks. I hated trailer living! Three years later we moved into a town house with wall-to-wall carpet, triple pane windows and a heated garage. In my heart I said," Thank you, Lord! I'll never live in a trailer ever again!" Well, that was not the Lord's plan.

In 2000 my husband answered the call into evangelism and after 17 years in Alaska we sold everything and moved into an RV permanently.

Another trailer, but this time no foundation under it. What if I had refused because I didn't like trailer living? Think of all the lives I would have been responsible for not hearing a message that would direct their life for the Lord.

> ***Luke 9:23...****If any man will come after me, let him deny himself and take up his cross daily, and follow me.*

I'm sure, like me...you want to hear the Lord say, *"Well done thou good and faithful servant. Thou hast been faithful over a few things...enter thou into the joy of the Lord."* **Matthew 25:20**

faithfulness- loyal, trustworthy, steadfast.

What a character quality! If you possess it, you will outshine them all! Proverbs is full of examples dealing with it. Take the time to read Proverbs 31:10-31 right now. It addresses every area that we should be faithful in as wives. I especially like verse 12,'She will do him good and not evil all the days of her life.' All means 'without exception. In every situation and on every day.'

meekness- instructing those that oppose themselves (I think we covered this in the previous chapter).

temperance- restraint or moderation.

The ability to say, 'No!' Many of us know when we should stop, but for some reason we can't find the discipline to do so. We have trouble walking away from a conversation, stopping that final statement, or turning from a temptation. Many times, this limits us from the work God wants to do with us. I can name a few areas I need some restraint, can you?

What a challenging list of character that is in the heart of God's **'Glorious'** Daughter.

One more thing...*Galatians 5:23* ends with, *'against such there is no law.'* You will never stand before God and have him say, 'You were just too joyful down there on earth. What were you thinking?' There is no quota. You can manifest them as much and as often as you want. They come from God and his resources are unlimited.

A little Homework...

   A. How would you describe the quantity of the fruit of the spirit you display at home?

      1. never
      2. rare
      3. occasional
      4. frequent
      5. constant

   B. What is one fruit of the Spirit that needs improvement in your personal life?

      1. What consequence or damage have you and your family suffered because of the lack of this spiritual fruit?

      2. List 2 steps that you can take to add this fruit in your personal life:

C. How often do you see answered prayer and spiritual victories in your life?

    1. never
    2. seldom
    3. sometimes
    4. frequently
    5. constantly

D. What is one way you can show sacrificial love to your family this week?

E. List one or two things that are stealing your joy? Take them to the Lord daily in prayer this week. Look for two ways to help the sunshine in your life. Thankfulness is a good place to start.

F. Is there something you want that God has said, 'No or wait?' Is He trying to do something, and you find yourself fighting him?

G. Are you easy to work with? Can your family testify that you have a submissive spirit? Give an example.

H. What dream or dreams are you refusing to surrender to the Lord?

I. List one thing you can become faithful in this year.

J. What do you need to say, 'No' to, that keeps you from growing spiritually?

Memory verse

Galatians 5:22,23...*But the fruit of the Spirit is love, joy, peace, longsuffering, gentleness, goodness, faith, meekness, temperance: against such there is no law.*

Glorious Within Her Heart

After - Action Report

We have just finished Part One of our journey to becoming 'glorious' daughters of the King. We started with our hearts and those first steps of growth that are needed in our lives. We have had many questions and challenges along the way. Goals have been set and we are striving to see changes in our walk, both in our private devotional life and our many daily relationships. So much has happened, and I feel it would be a great time for us to reflect on some of the decisions we have made. Good intentions can get swallowed up in our busy routines and so does information overload. We also don't want to get discouraged and quit.

During military action they have what is called a debriefing. This takes place directly after an assignment is accomplished. All those involved in the operation answer pertinent questions and give feedback so that correction can take place and they can do their job more efficiently. Both good and bad are discussed. This doesn't just happen during war time. It takes place after routine flights and practices.

I think it would be a great idea for us to do that also. We are going to have an *After-Action Report* after each part of our study together. This should enable us to check our progress and get back on track. Allowing us to see some rewards from our new habits that we have painstakingly added and redirect in the few things we started but have fallen by the wayside. This will help fuel the harder changes we may have to make. I encourage you to take the extra time to make this a productive lesson.

We will need to start this time with a heart-searching prayer, asking the Lord to speak to us and give Him permission to tear down any strongholds that are keeping us from being 'glorious'. You will need to get some paper and go back over the earlier lessons writing down your thoughts in the areas the Lord speaks to your heart. Read your answers to the many different questions and see what progress is taking place. Analyze your energy, methods and motives for any of the changes you are hoping to see. Prepare to roll your sleeves up and get to work!

> Dear Heavenly Father...
> Thank you for your great love for me and your continual working in my life. During the last few weeks I have come to the knowledge that my heart needs lots of work. I have habits and desires that I have allowed to control my life. Some of these have been recently brought to light and I want to see them changed into actions and attitudes that will bring you glory. Please help me to see myself the way you see me so that I can begin to hate what you hate and love what you love. Please help me and give me the strength to see this through. I will give you all the glory and praise!
> ...in Your Holy Name,
> Amen

A little Homework...

1. What were some of your goals from the previous five chapters? (see if you can list 8)

2. *How would you grade the results of the time invested in each of them? (put your grade after each goal above)*

      a. Highly profitable
      b. Things are moving in the right direction
      c. Neutral
      d. Feeling resistance
      f. Put little or no effort

3. *List the positive things you are enjoying or beginning to see because of your efforts?*

4. *What brought about the positive and negative results?*

5. *List three things you can do to change the negative results into positive ones?*

...a changed heart (dirty past)

This is my story...

Those drums, I can't sleep! When will they ever stop! So many bad memories.

I will never forget that day...poor little Avith. The screams from her mother as they tore her out of her arms, the drums drowned out the sounds of her cries as the priests marched up the path with the little helpless baby in the air. I couldn't look! I turned and hid my face in my mother's skirt. It wasn't long, and that awful smell of burning flesh was in the air.

What kind of god requires such a sacrifice? What kind of people choose an innocent child to die, so some battle can be won, the rain to fall or for a good crop?

I will never believe in god!!!

... ten years later... Whatever did god do for me? Nothing! This big house on the wall was all my idea and hard work. Being pretty and a little sassy, helped. Men loved that. They came crawling. They can't say no to me...they keep coming back. No one can deny how beautiful I am. Yes, some look at me with scorn...but I don't sacrifice my children or others' children to any god.

Can you guess who I am?

Rahab. Born and raised in Jericho a wicked idolatrous city. Joshua 2 says she was a harlot by profession and that she had a house on the wall...speaks of prominence and wealth.

Working in such a profession brought all the most recent news and gossip. It wasn't long before word about the children of Israel and their God came to her ears. The bondage of the Jews in Egypt was no secret. Slavery was a common practice in the world. However, the plagues and the great destruction of a nation by the hand of a God was a first. Hearing of these events brought fear in many hearts, Rahab being one of them.

This fear brought about a **Sanctified Heart** in Rahab. After hearing of the many accounts of this God and what he did, she began to see God for the first time. This was no idol made of stone or wood that she was accustomed to.

Soon the rumors of the Jews coming toward Jericho became common conversation. When the spies came into town, she knew she had to hear from them about their God. She hid them and in

Joshua 2:9 it says," I know that the Lord hath give you the land, and that your terror is fallen upon us". Verse 11 says, "The Lord your God, he is God in heaven above, and in earth beneath".

Hebrews 11:31..." By faith, the harlot Rahab perisheth not with them that believed not."

God was so good to us by not ending this story with a simple, 'She lived happily ever after'. He showed us His next step, the **Sanctified Heart**. In Joshua 6:24 it says that Rahab and all that she had dwelt in Israel. Her life changed and so did her heart. She learned about and began to follow this God that could save her and change her life. In fact, she changed so much that she caught the eye of a very influential man in Israel.

In Matthew 1:5 it says, Salmon, leader of the tribe of Benjamin married Rahab. Salmon begat Boaz of Rahab and Boaz and Ruth begat Obed, and Obed had Jesse and Jesse had David. She was in the lineage of the Messiah.

Last of all we see the **Strengthened Heart**. The third step in getting a 'Glorious' Heart. James 2:25 says, "was not Rahab the harlot justified by works?" There are so many benefits that can be enjoyed when we allow the Word of Christ to dwell in us richly.

Col. 3:16... Let the Word of Christ dwell in you richly in all wisdom; teaching and admonishing one another in psalms and hymns and spiritual songs, singing with grace in your hearts to the Lord.

a selfish heart...

This is my story...

I was the youngest daughter of a king. I enjoyed honey cakes and figs to my heart's desire. My clothes were gay and colorful as a princess' should be. Life in the palace was grand! Parties and fun on every hand. The stories, oh the stories! I heard many exciting tales while eavesdropping on the men as they recounted the events of the day, or the many jokes they played on one another.

Things really got exciting when Samuel the prophet came to worship with our family. The feasts and sacrifices on high holy days were the highlight of everyone's year. I, being a princess, had a first-class view of all the happenings. God seemed so real! No one could make the stories of our people come alive like Samuel. God spoke to him. Samuel went to God for my father, helping him make the right choices for the children of Israel.

Then, one day everything began to change...I'm not sure of all that happened, but my father, the king, came home from battle and he was never the same. He seemed to always be angry and even tried to kill my brother. I was afraid. This was not good. How could he continue being king acting like that? Then the rumors began to spread that God had removed my father and family from being king. He had chosen another man to be king. What could that mean? Me, a commoner? No way!

I started thinking... If I married the next king I would be 'queen'. I could have the next heir to the throne, and then, I would be the 'queen mother'. I would live the rest of my life in the palace.

Who am I?

Her father described her: I Samuel 18:21, "I will give him her, that she may be a snare to him." As her father he knew something about her that would lead to David's demise. Are you hiding something that could be your doom or a snare to someone you love?

She married the Great Psalmist of Israel – but obviously was not influenced by his life. Do you attend to the things of God but see no growth or victory over sin?

I Samuel 19:13... Michal took an image and laid it in the bed – she worshiped idols. Is there something you trust in other than the Lord? Your abilities, finances, good looks...

At the end of her life; Michal despised David. II Samuel 6:20... How glorious was the king of Israel today, who uncovered himself today in the eyes of the handmaids of his servants, as one of the vain fellows shamelessly uncovereth himself.

She was ashamed of the behavior of her husband and his worship of his God. She felt that his actions were unbecoming of a king. Is your pride keeping you from worshipping the Lord?

This seems to be the last straw, for David reproved her with a life of solitude. She brought about a curse on her life. She is a great example to us, allowing us to see the fruit of our unyielding hearts.

Despite all the good she enjoyed...

1. Lived in safety with no need or fear, pampered
2. Saw God prosper her father and nation
3. Worshipped with Samuel in the temple

Michal had a selfish and disrespectful heart. Are you doing good things, but not serving God?

If I were to ask you to write as many of the fruit of the Spirit you can think of and their meanings, or a list of the items we need to take off or put on, could you? But the real question is how many are seen in your life. Michal knew about Israel's God, but it's obvious she didn't know Him personally.

Philippians 4:13...I can do all things through Christ which strengtheneth me.

Part Two

Glorious Towards Her Husband

The Kings Daughter is all 'Glorious Within', is our thought for this book. We have defined **'glorious'** as being noble, excellent, very honorable...not a counterfeit. Our opening verse was;

> *Colossians 1:10...That ye might walk worthy of the Lord unto all pleasing, being fruitful in ever good work, and increasing in the knowledge of God.*

We have learned that the first place our King wants us to be **'glorious'** is in our Hearts.

> *Genesis 6:5,6...And God saw that the wickedness of man was great in the earth, and that every imagination of the thoughts of his heart was only evil continually. And it repented the Lord that he had made man on the earth and it grieved him at his heart.*

God was able not only to see mankind and his deeds, but he looked into his heart and saw the motives of his actions. What a thought! Our hearts can grieve God's heart. That means it can also bring Him joy. We don't picture the Creator of this universe feeling emotions from the way we live and think. Being that is so, I have a question for you, If your heart was the only heart that God was looking at right now...How would your heart affect His heart? Would he be grieved? Would he be angry? Would he be pleased?

Glorious Towards Her Husband

Chapter Five

Husbands

This brings up the relationship of marriage.

God's desire for companionship and fellowship caused him to create mankind much higher than all other creatures. We were created with a free will. Everything else operates on an inner time schedule or instinct. We get to choose what our heart chases after, who we fellowship with and what brings us joy. God was looking for that kind of close fellowship. This is the act of sharing one's heart and feelings. He wanted mankind to share in that fellowship by his own free will.

> **Genesis 1:27**...*So God created man in his own image, in the image of God created he him; male and female created he them.*
> **Genesis 3:8a**...*And they heard the voice of the Lord God walking in the garden in the cool of the day...*

Emotions, a desire to share, laughter and communication are a great need in our life. It sets us apart from the animal kingdom. God saw that Adam was lonely during the hours He was away. He tried sending the animals by for him to name and enjoy, but that only showed that he was the only creature that didn't have a companion.

Because of Adam's great need, Eve was created. God said it was not good for man to be alone. At the end of each day of creation, God said what He had created was 'good'. For the first time something was not 'good'. Something had to be done. Man would be worse off without a help meet.

> **Genesis 2:18**...*And the Lord God said, It is not good that the man should be alone; I will make him an help meet for him.*
> **Genesis 2:22-24**...*And the rib, which the Lord God had taken from man, made he a woman, and brought her unto the man. And Adam said, "This is now bone of my bones, and flesh of my flesh: she shall be called Woman, because she was taken out of Man."*

It is very interesting that God chose a rib to make a woman. First, He took something from man, meaning he is incomplete without it. He could have used anything. It also means we were made to fit together in a harmonious relationship.

Second, we came from his side. This gives us a picture of what God created us to do. We are to stay close to him, guard his life supporting organs and nestle under his strong arm for his protection. This world is hard! Our men go out there to provide for us. They are confronted with demanding bosses, worldly coworkers and a dog-eat-dog atmosphere. The devil has lots of temptations prepared for them. God meant for us to be his lover, guard and cheerleader. With him as our focus both parties are kept from the wiles of the devil.

And third, we were made from a bone. That means we are structural. We can do the many jobs he is unable or unwilling to do. He can put weight on us and we don't fall apart easily. We complete our husbands. We were created to help solve problems, not be a problem. It is not a 'sit on a shelf and look pretty' type of fix. It is a call to action and purpose.

God's plan was for a man to find satisfaction with his wife. They come home to their castle hoping to find peace, and a wife that is his queen, who has a way of making the toil of the day disappear.

    We are blessed to have four married children. Our second daughter Karen married a Floridian named Matt. During the day while he was gone to work, she was deeply concerned about the condition of the home. Working one shift a week as a critical care nurse and having two toddlers made life hectic. (Can you relate?) When Matt came home, she would be racing around frantically putting away laundry and picking up toys. She so wanted their home to be perfect and have it all together. It made Matt's first minutes at home stressful. Finally, one day Matt said to her," Karen, I'm not looking for a perfectly clean home. I just want to see my three girls (wife and 2 daughters) all happy and excited to see daddy, a good dinner, and clean clothes to wear to work."

    Do you meet the king of your castle with a list of frustrations from the day? Does your man have take-out or pizza several times a week instead of a home cooked meal? Is he having to work overtime to pay for the 'little extras' that you have to have to keep YOU happy? Does he need to come home and put his apron on and do YOUR job? Ladies, why do you think your man goes to work 8-10 hours a day? He works so you can stay home and take care of the things at home. Is your home clean and full of laughter? Are YOU training your children to obey? Can your man count on having clean laundry and a hot meal at the end of the day?

> ***Genesis 2:24-25...****Therefore shall a man leave his father and his mother, and shall cleave unto his wife: and they shall be one flesh. And they were both naked, the man and his wife, and were not ashamed.*
> ***Hebrews 13:4...****Marriage is honorable in all, and the bed undefiled.*

God created marriage to unite us in a deep, intimate fellowship. It is to be shared with one person our whole life through. Believe it or not, this is a need both parties have and benefit from. Remember those vows? In sickness and in health, for richer or poorer. Can I use the term unconditional? Long after the honeymoon is over, and the trials of life come upon us? Without mommy or daddy interfering and after that first disagreement? This is one of the tasks that is very important for us to protect. We so want to make them pay when we get hurt. The silent treatment, tears, slamming things, or withholding ourselves till we get what we want. Ladies, that is a sin!

> *I Corinthians 7:2-5...Nevertheless, to avoid fornication, let every man have his own wife, and let every woman have her own husband. Let the husband render unto the wife due benevolence: and likewise also the wife unto the husband. The wife hath not power of her own body, but the husband: and likewise also the husband hath not power of his own body, but the wife. Defraud ye not one the other, except it be with consent for a time, that ye may give yourselves to fasting and prayer; and come together again, that Satan tempt you not for your incontinency.*
>
> *Ephesians 4:26...Be ye angry, and sin not: let not the sun go down upon your wrath:*

How is your love life? Now I'm meddling, you say? God knew that life and our own selfishness would bring about divisions with our husbands. These divisions would create a big need that could cause one or both of us to sin. Intimacy is a need. You think that men are the ones with such a need, you are so wrong. There is big business for romance books and movies. What drives that business? Women do! We can't get our fill of romance. We enjoy being chased and courted and, in some cases, do the chasing.

Part of being 'glorious' towards our husband is intimacy. It's time to take charge of this necessary part of our marriage. Everyone will benefit. So, get back to chasing your man and don't let anything come between you and him.

A little Homework…

   A. How often do you pray for your husband?

1. Never
2. Rarely
3. Occasionally
4. Frequently
5. Constantly

   B. Make a list of five things you can pray for your husband. Begin to pray daily for him that God would bless, guide and protect him.

   C. With your free will what is your heart chasing after?

1. Possessions
2. Honor or reputation
3. Career
4. Happiness or a good time
5. Making others happy
6. Growing and pleasing the Lord

   D. What kind of influence are you to your husband?

1. Cold, distant, and hateful
2. Worldly
3. Self- absorbed
4. Neutral
5. Godly

E. What two things can you do to bring your influence up a notch.

F. What can your husband count on when he walks through the door after a long day at work?

G. List three things you can do to make his homecoming better.

Suggestions: Start getting your home ready for him two hours before he walks through the door. Turn your electronics and social media off and set your book down. Get dinner cooking...crock pot meals are great! Spend a little time getting ready yourself. Sometimes this means a change of clothes. Have a group clean up time half an hour out.

Memory verse

Genesis 2:18...*And the LORD God said, It is not good that the man should be alone; I will make him an help meet for him.*

Glorious Towards Her Husband

Chapter Six
Our Goal 'Happiness!'

What is the ultimate goal that you are trying to achieve? **To be happy**! We are all making plans to be '**happy**'. We have high expectations in this life, but all lead to **happiness**. Our marriage is no exception. We want to be loved, satisfied emotionally, cared for, and attain a standard of living that we set.

No man can do that!

> *Proverbs 16:9...A man's heart deviseth his way: but the Lord directeth his steps.*
> *Proverbs 14:12...There is a way that seemeth right unto a man, but the end thereof are the ways of death.*

Solomon had a lot to say about the choices we make and the consequences of those choices. Our hearts decide what is best for us right now, or what it will get us in the near future. We are short sighted and tend to think very selfishly. In the long run the happiness is short lived and the casualty list along the way is devastating.

Our expectations for happiness go right into our marriage. We find Mr. Right and can imagine a life of bliss. Very little thought has gone into the events of the future, his needs or happiness or what the Lord wants. We will stop at nothing to make our dreams come true.

One big problem...Our flesh is never satisfied. After the honeymoon we start decorating and buying things for the house. When that's done, we want to show it off. Then comes vacation, the new car, what about the yard and a baby. Now you need a bigger house and the whole thing starts all over again.

The reality of someone else making us happy is a dream. We give up on our husbands to satisfy us and we escape to romance books and love stories. We get carried away with the 'thrill'. We forget the book or movie ends and leaves out what happens during the rest of their life. (not to mention the many deleted scenes that were left out to produce the 'happily ever after' finish.)

Our husbands can't compare to that! This only makes it harder for them to fulfill the intimacy need in our life. The 'thrill' we get from our imagination steals what we could have had that is real and lasting.

The Bible speaks about a Foolish Woman and the end of chasing and satisfying thrills in her life.

> ***Proverbs 14:1...Every wise woman buildeth her house: but the foolish plucketh it down with her hands.***

To pluck means to tear things up and pull them down. It makes me think of butchering chickens. In the fall we would set aside a Saturday for butchering chickens. It was a very messy and stinky job. The worst was lowering a dead chicken by the feet into a kettle of boiling water and then plucking those stinky, wet feathers off. You had to get every little quill. It would be several weeks before we got over the smell and could enjoy fried chicken again. It was a job that took focus. Like the foolish woman, we would tear what was beautiful off the birds. All the way down to the skin.

The foolish woman is using her hands to destroy what God has given her to build and enjoy. She is not interested in God's way, what the Bible says, or any spiritual counsel. She is unteachable, highly selfish and unwilling to put the work needed into her home. She is unwilling to change her goals and dreams to make her marriage a success, least of all try to figure out what her husband's needs are or how to make him happy.

Right now, you are thinking of the sacrifices you have made in your marriage and counting his mistakes and those selfish decisions that were an 'inconvenience' at best. I have found that staring at these things has not made my marriage any happier. In fact, it seems to steal my joy, affecting other areas of my life. On top of that, it doesn't make the problem any better. Here are a few verses that have helped me through the years.

> ***Proverbs 17:9**...He that covereth a transgression seeketh love; but he that repeateth a matter separateth very friends.*
> ***Proverbs 19:11**...The discretion of a man deferreth his anger; and it is his glory to pass over a transgression.*
> ***I Peter 4:8**...And above all things have fervent charity among yourselves: for charity shall cover the multitude of sins.*

The Lord knew that we would have some major needs in our marriage relationships. Giving one another the space to grow up and fail and then press on is hard to do, but necessary. Remember the first time he came home to pink t-shirts, or you burnt dinner? What about that purchase you failed to record in the checkbook ledger and the account went in the red. Or you forgot to pay a bill, or worse yet, mail an in-law's birthday card? We have all made these and other mistakes. Shouldn't we extend some mercy and forgiveness?

We all know that life is always adjusting. As our family grows the workload does also. It will be several years till our children will be able to help carry the load. Until then, Moms carry the brunt of the responsibility. The foolish woman is unable or unwilling to grow in character. She doesn't want to grow the fruit of the spirit in her life, which will allow her to face the challenges of each day. All she sees is that she is missing out on the life she dreamed of having. Her thoughts are on pleasing self. Her family is a big burden. She is unconcerned at the cost necessary to live her selfish life. Some have lost their marriages, children, joy or testimonies. What unnecessary losses.

Years ago, in Alaska, a young woman, we will call Beth, got saved. She had two small children and a husband. Being a first-generation Christian, she had no good role models. She had a strong desire to be a Godly mom and wife, and see her husband come to the Lord. I invited her to come over and observe my homeschooling family of six and how we ordered our home. She came at ten in the morning, had lunch and left around four. I didn't require anything from her. The day was pretty normal. Her parting comment was," I want what you have, but it's too much of me to give." Out the door she went. After that she spent many years being with silly women who tore down their homes. About ten years later she saw her mistake and began to build her home. Her husband got saved and they became faithful to church and got involved in ministry as a family.

Like Beth, are you saying, 'That's too much of me to give' in an area of your life? If you decide to do it your way, the casualty list will be heavy. Are you sure that what you think will make you happy is worth the loss of a husband, children and your testimony?

A little Homework...

   A. How often do you read a devotional, missionary story, or spiritual help book?

        1. Never
        2. Rarely
        3. Occasionally
        4. Frequently
        5. Constantly

   *Make a habit of reading one a month for a whole year and see how they influence your life.

   B. Fast this month from romance books and shows. Invest in your marriage/love life.

C. Look deep in your life and list some of the selfish and foolish choices or things you are doing that are destroying your home.

    1.
    2.
    3.
    4.

D. List the four things your husband would say were destroying your home.

    1.
    2.
    3.
    4.

E. What things have you lost or are losing because of those choices?
    1.
    2.
    3.
    4.

F. What three things can you do to stop plucking down your home and the relationships in it?

    1.
    2.
    3.

Memory verse

Proverbs 14:1*...Every wise woman buildeth her house: but the foolish plucketh it down with her hands.*

Chapter Seven

Love's Goal

We have identified our goal in marriage, **Happiness.** Let's look at Love's Goal. We know that love comes from God, and his love has no end. He extended that love to us at Calvary. We will refer to this as, '**Vertical Love.**' Love that travels from God to us or us to God. Before we knew we had a need, his death on the cross was planned. We certainly didn't deserve it. We have perfected the art of living sinful lives without the guilt. Justifying the littlest transgression. Our hearts are so prone to wander, and, at any cost, we look to please self.

> **John...3:16** *For God so loved the world, that he gave his only begotten Son, that whosoever believeth in him should not perish, but have everlasting life.*
> **Romans 5:8**...*But God commendeth his live toward us, in that, while we were yet sinners, Christ died for us.*

If you could think of a word to describe this kind of love, what would it be? Moms display this love with their young children. We deal with teething and nighttime feedings when we really need our sleep. The spilled milk and the, 'I need to go potty!' where there aren't facilities available, are classic examples. Squeezing the routine of the day to make all practices and doctor appointments are all typical examples of that kind of love. God practices this 'Vertical' love non-stop to mankind every day. How are you doing with returning that love? The most beneficial love goes both ways.

I was talking to a family member some time ago and they were complaining how they haven't heard from another member in a long time. I asked them, "When was the last time you called them?" Of course, they felt the other party should be the one to call. I replied, "Last time I checked the phone lines go both ways." We can be so short sighted.

Love's Goal is Sacrifice...

Sacrifice is the act of giving up something that you want to keep, especially for the sake of a better cause.

Christ practiced this kind of love 'vertically' toward us. When we spend time with him and serve him, we are returning that sacrificial love. Now let's look at the sacrificial love we share with one another. This is the '**Horizontal**' view of love. It travels from person to person. It happens intentionally. It will cost you something and take time. Remember when you set your eyes on your husband? Everyone else disappeared. You began sitting together and glancing at one another across the room. You rearranged your schedule and did things with him that you had no interest in, but he was there, and that made all the difference in the world. This is called being 'twitter-pated'. It's the beginning of a relationship based on love. Then he asked the million-dollar question and you said, "Yes!" It wasn't long after that things came up and you had to graduate from love that brought you happiness, to sacrificial love.

We can't look at love without going to the love chapter of the Bible, **I Corinthians 13**. It is a very in-depth description of sacrificial love.

verse 1... Though I speak with the tongues of men and of angels, and have not charity, I am become as sounding brass, or a tinkling cymbal.

Words without love, are nothing. Remember those school days when the 'in group of girls' came to you with sweet words and smiles. For a time, you were in...a short time. Then they got what they wanted, and you were the one they laughed at over their shoulders. They had no interest in your wellbeing. They used you. Has that ever happened to you? It is an awful feeling. Have you ever done that to someone else?

Relationships are lost many times by how we speak and our goals behind the conversation. We need to be genuine in our relationships so in the end we can be a witness for Christ. If someone knows that you care for them, you can tell them very hard things and they will listen. Why? Because they know you have their best interests in mind. But this is a relationship that has had some investment. You have willingly put yourself out for them or came to their aid. Your words of friendship have been backed up, not with intentions, but with actions.

Our husbands should be at the top of that sacrificial list. Do you say, 'I love you!' with the feelings to back it up? Do your words build him up or tear him down? Is your husband embarrassed by your condescending, complaining conversation both in private and public? By our daily actions of putting his needs and wants above our own, we win his heart, and he has no need of spoil.

> ***Proverbs 31:11**...The heart of her husband doth safely trust in her, so that he shall have no need of spoil.*
> ***verse 2**...And though I have the gift of prophecy, and understand all mysteries, and all knowledge; and though I have all faith, so that I could remove mountains, and have not charity, I am nothing.*

Works without love, are nothing. Life gets busy and we fall into a routine. Children, homeschooling, part time ministries or jobs, and the normal demands of running a household leave us little free time. Be careful, we don't want our homes to be all about the mission and not the people in it. Part of that routine should be confirming your love to the ones that mean the most to you. The ones under your roof. Laughter and a loving touch are important ingredients. I know that our men are tough, but don't leave them out. Their lives can be just as hectic as ours. After working that eight to ten-hour day they are tired. Make sure he knows he has something to come home to. Every day, not just when you are going out. The devil has someone out there prepared to steal his heart and we make that easy to happen when we do not treat our husbands with the love and adoration they deserve. My husband likes Tapioca pudding; thus, I keep the supplies for it on hand and make it rather frequently. This is one of the ways I demonstrate my love to him. What is something your husband likes that you can make a habit of doing for him?

verse 3...And though I bestow all my goods to feed the poor, and though I give my body to be burned, and have not charity, it profiteth me nothing.

    Life without love is nothing. We are so busy doing! I am fond of Anne of Green Gables. I like the quote from Aunt Josephine to Anne concerning her lack of boyfriends at college, "Make a little time for romance, nothing in the world makes up for it."

    My husband and I are empty nesters and recently celebrated our 34th anniversary. We are enjoying the best years of our married life! There have been tough times, misunderstandings, struggles in our ministry, negative family influences, health issues and so much more. Yes, there have been times when one or both of us wanted to walk. Living with an imperfect person is not easy! Wait! I'm not perfect either! But without that sacrificial love we exercised earlier, we would be missing out on these.

The Best Years of our Lives!

> *Proverbs 14:4...Where no oxen are, the crib is clean: but much increase is by the strength of the ox.*

The ox is very strong and can get much work done quickly. But they require lots of feed and being picked up after. Have you ever thought, "I could do better without him!" The financial burdens and workplace are a heavy load to carry but God has called our men to such a task. Without him I would have to go to work outside of the home, in probably a lost environment. My children would live in that world of being transplanted from one atmosphere to another, stepmom, dad and siblings. I would have to protect myself from the men out there looking to take advantage of me. Finances would always be tight. I would have to raise my kids by myself, and I would miss out on the many things we enjoy doing together.

> *Verses 4-8a...Charity suffereth long, and is kind; charity envieth not; charity vaunteth not itself, is not puffed up, Doth not behave itself unseemly, seeketh not her own, is not easily provoked, thinketh no evil; Rejoiceth not in iniquity, but rejoiceth in the truth; Beareth all things, believeth all things, hopeth all things, endureth all things. Charity never faileth:*

Sixteen things or qualities of true love. These are the unending qualities we need to extend to our husbands if we are to be 'glorious' towards them and pleasing to the Lord. Notice there are no qualifications of when to use them. It seems to assume that we should be living this way all the time. True charity is totally 'sacrificial' because it isn't based on getting something in return.

> *John 14:15...If ye love me, keep my commandments.*

Charity is love with work gloves on. It is not in getting, but in giving.

You come to love, not by finding the perfect person, but by seeing an imperfect person, perfectly.
...Sam Keen

A little Homework...

    A. List five intentional ways that you can express love to your husband.

    B. What is your husband's love language? (The **Five Love Languages** is a good book to start with)

        1. Physical Touch
        2. Acts of Service
        3. Quality Time
        4. Words of Affirmation
        5. Receiving Gifts

C. If your husband was to rate your love for him, which would he choose?

   1. Minimal
   2. Conditional
   3. Fairly frequently
   4. When things are going well
   5. Constant and genuine

D. Think back on this last month and write down any words or actions that tore down your man. Bring them to the Lord and ask him to forgive you. Figure out what you need to do to change these to positive inputs in his life.

E. Read I Corinthians 13

F. List the 16 qualities of True Love in verses 4-8a

Memory verse

Proverbs 31:12...She will do him good and not evil all the days of her life.

Glorious Towards Her Husband

Chapter Eight

Yielding to Love's Goal

We ended our last study with this saying from Sam Keen: You come to love, not by finding the perfect person. But by seeing an imperfect person perfectly.

Our goal of happiness is only realized when we yield to love's goal, sacrifice. This is a truth that we would probably agree on, but that will not give you a happy marriage. It is more than simply acknowledging what we need to do, it is doing it. It is taking the steps 'personally' for this to happen every day, when we feel like it or not, if we see things progressing or not.

First, let's look at a few contrasts to this 'Glorious and Virtuous' woman.

> ***Proverbs 19:13**...The contentions of a wife are a continual dropping.*
> ***Proverbs 21:9**...It is better to dwell in a corner of the house top, than with a brawling woman in a wide house.*
> ***Proverbs 21:19**...It is better to dwell in the wilderness, than with a contentious and an angry woman.*
> ***Proverbs 25:24**...It is better to dwell in the corner of the house top, than with a brawling woman and in a wide house.*
> ***Proverbs 27:15**...A continual dropping in a rainy day and a contentious woman are alike.*

Do you see what I see? Our conversation and attitude have a big say in the atmosphere of our home. When it goes downhill, well, everyone wants to hide. Their home, a place of safety and comfort, has now become a war zone. Who is responsible for this place called home? We are. Let's identify some of these words so we can be aware of them and start purging them from our lives and homes.

<u>contention</u>: argument, contest, debate, strife, and struggle
<u>brawling:</u> fight, skirmish, scuffle, exchange blows, wrestle
<u>angry</u>: strong resentment, wrathful

WOW! That is awful! No wonder everyone was running away. Living with someone who is combatant wears you down and has the power to steal joy from your life. 'Continual dropping in a rainy day' is how it's described. Is there something you have been 'harping' about getting fixed at home? Or is there something your man has done, or not done, that you won't forgive him for and keep bringing up? Our men work hard and deserve better. The devil has prepared temptations on every side, and we need to guard him. Providing an atmosphere of peace and acceptance is one good way to do that. Does he dread coming home? Let's become glorious and change the atmosphere of our homes.

> ***Proverbs 14:1**...Every wise woman buildeth her house: but the foolish plucketh it down with her hands.*

Build and pluck are action words. You can define which woman you are by what action is yours. You can't do both. They are total opposite. Better yet, which would your husband and children say is yours?
   I want to introduce you to a friend of mine. She has it all together. I mean, she is Super Woman! A true hero! She has been a great encouragement to me. I'm sure you have heard of her. She is the Proverbs 31 Woman. If you read through the

book of Proverbs every month (there is a chapter for each day), you get to read and hear her wise counsel and see the wonderful rewards her sacrificial life brings. Not just to her, but everyone who comes in contact with her. Let's look at her words of wisdom and see if we can glean some of her habits and attitudes.

> ***Proverbs 31:10...Who can find a virtuous woman? for her price is far above rubies.***

Virtuous means righteous, clean living, pure, and exemplary. It is also a reference used to speak about an honored military soldier, one who has shown great character and strength in very adverse conditions. Solomon mentions that this kind of woman is very difficult to find, and when one does find her, you will have to pay a great price to obtain her. The rest of the chapter gives us an inside look at this highly decorated women.

> ***vs. 11...The heart of her husband doth safely trust in her, so that he shall have no need of spoil.***

Trust is firm belief in the reliability, truth, ability, or strength of someone or something.
What a word! The first thing we do is look around and see 'who' I can trust. Right? The Proverb 31 Woman seems to say, "He can trust me no matter what". Even if he doesn't deserve it. I have his back. I have every area of his life protected. He is the 'priority' in my life.
Let's list a few of these areas: Testimony, finances, health, clean home and clothing, child training, aiding in his ministries, in-laws and much, much more. I think of Abigail in I Samuel 25. David sent men to Nabal, Abigail's husband, to receive a gift for the protection of his flocks and herds in the wilderness. Nabal turned them away roughly so David was going to kill him and his family. Abigail heard about it and prepared a gift and

went to meet David. She bowed herself before him and asked for mercy for herself, her husband and family. Wow! What an example of this verse. Are there areas in your husband's life that he needs you to step up and make him look good? That is exactly what verse 11 means. We make our husband look good.

It mentions his heart, his emotions, desires and dreams. God created them with a strong romance and ego need. Do you satisfy the physical needs your man has? They are very vulnerable in this area. They need constant touch and words of affirmation. Believe it or not, we need to keep the honey in our marriages. This area of our marriage should never be used as a bargaining chip. 'No need of spoil.' We also should be known as their biggest personal cheer leader. We need to constantly look for ways to build them.

> **vs.12...She will do him good and not evil all the days of her life.**

The word 'good' is used to describe the outcome of the decisions we make. Do our attitudes and decisions bring about a 'favorable' look on our husbands? It doesn't say that it will take no work on our part. We must 'do' something and continue to 'do' it. It's going to take energy and effort. We choose the outcome of the happiness in our homes by the decisions we make and the things we do.

> ***Proverbs 31:13-22, 24, 27*** *She seeketh wool, and flax, and worketh willingly with her hands. She is like the merchants' ships; she bringeth her food from afar. She riseth also while it is yet night, and giveth meat to her household and a portion to her maidens. She considereth a field, and buyeth it: with the fruit of her hands she planteth a vineyard. She girdeth her loins with strength, and strengtheneth her arms. She*

perceiveth that her merchandise is good: her candle goeth not out by night. She layeth her hands to the spindle, her hands hold the distaff. She stretcheth out her hand to the poor; yea, she reacheth forth her hands to the needy. She is not afraid of the snow for her household, for all her household are clothed with scarlet. She maketh herself coverings of tapestry; her clothing is silk and purple.... She maketh fine linen, and selleth it; and delivereth girdles unto the merchant.... She looketh well to the ways of her household, and eateth not the bread of idleness.

There is no doubt that this Proverbs 31 woman is very industrious. Always on the lookout for a deal. She knows quality when she sees it, and value. She has an eye to improve on something, thus bringing home a return that adds to the household finances. Her husband can trust her with large sums of money. She is not afraid of work and has an eye for investments that will provide for the future.

In our modern day this would probably transfer to one who checks secondhand stores and end of season sales. Shopping the sales ads at the local grocery store and going early on the mark down days to scarf up the sale items. Planting a garden. Having an in-home business, like alterations or sewing, giving piano lessons, dog breeding, childcare, caring for elderly, house cleaning, refurbishing furniture or a distant internet job. Whatever it is, it doesn't take away from the family and what needs to be done at home. What a goal to shoot for!

A few words stick out to me:

1. <u>worketh willingly with her hands</u>...are you known for complaining or excusing the many tasks that you are responsible for? Do you disappear when there is work to be done?

2. *riseth while it is still night*...this means getting up early, before others and the chaos begins. If you were to get up a half hour earlier would that make a positive difference in your home?

3. *Her candle goeth not out by night*...she is productive at all hours. She has a plan for each day, and she works her plan. Not easily side-tracked and ready for the unexpected things life throws her way. Make a plan for each day this week. Devotions, meals, shopping lists and trips, errands, chores, even play time.

4. *Stretcheth out her hand to the poor and needy*...she sees the need beyond her family and takes the time to meet it. She makes the effort to lift someone else's burden. Not church related or of those who can repay the favor.

5. *Eateth not the bread of idleness*...how many hours do you waste during any normal day? It's amazing how quickly time can slip away. Electronics is one of the big wasters. Itemize your day and see where you spend your time.

> ***Proverbs 31:23...Her husband is known in the gates, when he sitteth among the elders of the land.***

Because of her input into her husband's life he is with the elders and wise men of the land. *She is making her man look good!* Did you notice that she is nowhere near where the decisions are being made? She can do all that without being seen or heard from.

We tend to minimize our task as homebuilders and look for ways to get involved in something more visible and with what we consider productive. Now don't misunderstand me, we are needed to fill many roles in our homes, churches and communities. They just shouldn't take away from our first God given responsibility. The Proverbs 31 Woman had many, many things she did, in many areas of life, but never at the expense of her home.

> ***Proverbs 31:25,26***...*Strength and honour are her clothing; and she shall rejoice in time to come. She openeth her mouth with wisdom; and in her tongue is the law of kindness.*

Look at the strength this woman has! Anyone who has been able to master their tongue has conquered a big one. How would you fare if you were graded on the words you spoke? Could it be said that you have the law of kindness in your tongue? When you speak what comes out? Words of wisdom, with grace and honour? All too often I fall for the trap of being funny and then wish there was something not said. Let's endeavor to put a guard on our conversation. Like Thumper's mom says, "If you can't say something nice, don't say anything at all."

> ***Proverbs 31:28-31***...*Her children arise up and call her blessed; her husband also, and he praiseth her. Many daughters have done virtuously, but thou excellest them all. Favour is deceitful, and beauty is vain: but a woman that feareth the Lord, she shall be praised. Give her of the fruit of her hands; and let her own works praise her in the gates.*

A little Homework...
A. By your actions, how would your children describe your attitude towards your husband?

1. combative and confrontational
2. critical and manipulative
3. Neutral and disattached
4. Frequently supportive
5. Loving and faithfully supportive

B. *Make a plan for the week. Be sure and plan meals, school or homework, shopping and errands, devotions, chores and fun time. Let's keep track of our time and see where we can redeem a few hours.*

C. *When your husband walks into your home, what spiritual 'fragrance' do you greet him with?*

    1. Repulsive and Rotten
    2. Unpleasant
    3. Sterile and Neutral
    4. Fresh
    5. Sweet, loving and affectionate

D. *When your husband makes a decision that you disagree with, what word best describes your immediate response?*

    1. Confrontational
    2. Manipulative
    3. Neutral
    4. Flexible
    5. Supportive

E. *If your husband were to evaluate your fulfillment of a Proverbs 31 Woman, how would he grade you?*

    1. F
    2. D
    3. C
    4. B
    5. A

F. *Give me at least three reasons why you chose that answer and what can you do to get a higher score?*

G. List some of the things you have been harping on, or complaining about. Go to the Lord in prayer asking for forgiveness and give them to him and his perfect will. (I found that I had to do this more than once before I saw victory in my life.)

H. Write down the definitions for the following words: contentious, brawling and angry.

I. How is your love life? What 2 things can you do to improve it?

J. Keep a record of your time every day this week. Find what is robbing you from doing those things you know that you need to do.

K. What are two Proverbs 31 habits that are missing from your life that your husband needs from you?

   1. What consequence or damage has resulted because of these missing habits?

   2. List two steps for both that you can take to instill this habit into your marriage relationship:

Memory verse

Proverbs 31:11... *The heart of her husband doth safely trust in her, so that he shall have no need of spoil.*

Glorious Towards Her Husband

After - Action Report

Can you imagine... it is time for our second After Action Report!

We cannot become a 'glorious' daughter of the King if we do not Yield to Love's Goal in our marriage. The promise of happily ever after is only pretend. One of our daughters after being married a short time called and said," I didn't think I was selfish, until after I got married!" Can you relate?

Let's get ready to review our progress from the earlier four lessons. Start with the first set of questions in becoming 'glorious' towards our Husbands. Take notes on the decisions you made, the progress you have seen, and the lessons learned. How have you fared with the goals you set? Are you happy with the energy you put into each new habit? Did you feel that your attitude was pleasing to the Lord? What would you change? Be sure and list the good things you are seeing and thank the Lord for His grace and blessings.

A little Homework...

    A. *How would God evaluate your relationship with your husband:*
        1. little bit of heaven on earth
        2. good
        3. improving
        4. holding
        5. needs improvement
        6. neglected

    B. *What is the definition of sacrifice?*

    C. *What would be two areas that have slipped through the cracks and two things you can do to get the victory in each of these areas?*

D. List three things that you have put into your marriage since you began these lessons and what benefits you are enjoying?

E. Read I Corinthians 13 and Proverbs 31:13-22, 24, 27.

F. Pick three things from these verses you would like to see in your life.

- What 2 steps can you take to accomplish this and what fruit you are hoping to see grow?

G. List three opposites that you and your husband have and how they make you stronger as a team?

Take the results of this study to the Lord in private prayer. Thank him for what He is doing in your life and marriage. Ask Him to forgive you and help you to grow into the 'glorious' wife that you see in His word.

Memory verse

Genesis 2:18*...And the Lord God said, "It is not good that the man should be alone; I will make an help meet for him."*

A Name to be Chosen...by Cheryl Sutton

"Do you go by your husband's last name? "queried the car dealer. I just stared at him with my mouth slightly open. I finally replied that I did and that I did so with great joy. He proceeded to tell me that many married women refuse to use their husband's last mane. That started a process of thought on the blessings of belonging to someone. As a wife I belong to my husband. I carry his last name and benefit from his protection. As a Christian I belong to Christ. I carry His name and His protection. A woman who resents carrying her husband's last name must be a foolish woman indeed, but the woman who resents carrying the name of Christ is not only foolish, but a fool.

In this day of women's liberation many women are deceived by the devil's lie that their "independence" is important. What they do not know is that kind of independence is only bondage. Being lawfully and gladly bound to a man in a husband-and-wife relationship is real independence. Independence to be what God intended me to be. As a woman I do not have to depend upon my fainting strength to sustain me, but, rather, I can lean on my husband and allow him to be the leader and to carry the burden of responsibility that I was never intended to carry. Real womanly strength comes in submission-submission to Jesus Christ and then to her own husband. A woman's strength is demonstrated when she upholds her husband in prayer and in decisions that he makes. That strength takes character. Flaunting rights and independence does not demand character. Instead, it shows a lack of it. Solomon said, "A good name is rather to be chosen than great riches," and what better names could a woman have than those of a God-fearing husband and of her Savior. I am proud to carry both.

Part Three

Glorious Within Her Heritage

We have been developing the topic of being 'Glorious' daughters of the King. Our goal is to become more noble, excellent and very honorable. Our first area we considered becoming 'glorious' was within our hearts. We looked at the Spiritual Heart and our need to trust the Lord as Saviour. We moved to the Surrendered Heart and saw that we have habits and ideas that we need to abandon and put off. Lastly, we looked at Strengthening our Hearts. Growing and putting on attitudes and actions that define us as Daughters of the King. Thus, fulfilling our goal of becoming *'Glorious within our Hearts'*.

The next area we looked at was becoming *'Glorious' toward our Husbands*. God's goal in creating man was to enjoy 'Fellowship'. A desire for both parties to have a close personal relationship. Unfortunately, we turned that around and made it all about us. Which led to our goal-'Happiness.' Only finding happiness when our goals, dreams and desires are met. We learned that True Love's Goal is 'Sacrifice'. Putting the needs and happiness of others above our own. It is waking up in the morning with the goal of seeing those you love smile.

Proverbs 31:28-31 shows the fruit of that kind of Sacrifice,

> *Her children arise up, and call her blessed; her husband also, and he praiseth her. Many daughters have done virtuously, but thou excellest them all. Favour is deceitful and beauty is vain: but a woman that feareth the LORD, she shall be praised. Give her of the fruit of her hands; and let her own works praise her in the gates.*

Glorious Within Her Heritage

Chapter Nine

The word 'Mother' has many facets, but one main purpose. Our ultimate goal is to instill Godly character and discipline in our children, so that they can be the next: witnessing neighbor or coworker, sacrificial giver, faithful church member, nursery worker, pianist or vocalist, choir director, missionary, pastor, politician, godly mother or father, Sunday school teacher, and the list could go on. Our goal is not to get them potty trained or through the 3rd grade…but to equip them to be used by God.

> ***Deuteronomy 6:5-7**…And thou shalt love the Lord thy God with all thine heart, and with all thy soul, and with all thy might. And these words, which I command thee this day, shall be in thine heart: And thou shalt teach them diligently unto thy children, and shalt talk of them when thou sittest in thine house, and when thou walkest by the way, and when thou liest down, and when thou risest up.*

Look at those descriptive words! Teach, talk, bind and write. That doesn't sound like it just happens by chance. We, as mothers, need to know what we are to teach and how to weave it into our conversation during life's many situations. We can't do that if we don't love the Lord with all our heart, soul and might. We are responsible, just like our children, for the preaching and teaching we hear. How much of it do we actually live out and model ourselves? When was the last time you visited the altar after a message? Conviction no longer tugs at our hearts and we can't remember the last time we had victory over sin. How can we expect our children to be used of the Lord when we refuse to learn and obey Him?

If you think that is rough, the Lord tells us how we are to do that. Diligently. (Meaning at all times or relentlessly!) Diligence is like that sentry on guard duty. Everybody is busy with life, resting in the fact that the sentry is alert and watching. He gives warning and directions that everyone is depending on. He cannot afford to get side-tracked with what he wants right now. He is living for the safety of others. The punishment in time of war for falling asleep or not being at your post was death. This job is one of great reasonability. There are so many things this world is offering our children and we need to sound the alarm. If you were to analyze your words or actions this last week, how many of them were instructive in teacher your children Deuteronomy 6:5-7? How many were not necessary or destructive in nature? Are you a diligent sentry over your children's lives? Life is busy, but this is a vitally important job of training our children the principles in His Word. We are God's watchmen.

'When' is also one of the instructions mentioned in this verse. While sitting, lying down, and waking up. That doesn't seem to leave any position out. In other words, in everything we do and the attitudes that accompany those actions. A few things that helped me live this precept in my home was having Patch the Pirate, Odyssey and Your Story Hour C.D.s available. One was always in the van and playing. We loved singing the songs together. Each of our children had their own player and as soon as school and chores were done you could hear a different story or music wherever kids were found. It was not uncommon for someone to spread the word that it was so and so's favorite song or part and they would all come running. I purchased many missionary stories and used them for schoolbook reports and read many of them aloud before bed.

How will I ever accomplish all of this, you say? One step at a time. I encourage moms to build a pyramid of the things in their lives with the most important tasks at the top. All of us have a limit to our strength and endurance level. This will grow as you go along. There will be some things you will have to eliminate from your life for a while. I love to sew, but for many years my sewing only consisted of mending. Home schooling with six children, starting a church in Alaska and assisting in our home business left little spare time. Others of us need to learn to manage our time more wisely and pick up a ministry or service for the Lord. We need to be able to show are children how to serve and sacrifice for the Lord. They see our joy and begin to get involved. One of the little tricks that helped me redeem the time was a bird clock we received from my in-laws. Every hour a different bird would sing. This got my attention, and I would look around the house to see where and what my kids were doing, choose a task to accomplish that hour and check if things were progressing in the direction I wanted. This helped my home to run more smoothly and less time was wasted.

This is no simple job! It is going to take commitment and wisdom that only comes from the Lord. It begins with you being in love with your Saviour. You will have to be walking every step of the way with His Word shedding light on the direction you should go. Sometimes it is so dark we only see the path at our feet. While at other times we get a look at several decisions and turns ahead. Wherever you are in the process of parenting you need strength that comes from above.

Psalm 119:105...Thy word is a lamp unto my feet, and a light unto my path.
Matthew 5:13,14...Ye are the salt of the earth: but if the salt have lost his savour, wherewith shall it be salted? it is thenceforth good for nothing, but to be cast out, and to be trodden under foot of men. Ye are the light of the world. A city that is set on an hill cannot be hid.

My goal for my children was to prepare them to go beyond me and my husband for the Lord. I wanted them to be the salt and light spoken about in these verses. I wanted them to change this world, not simply fit in or accept it.

I love to share this illustration with Moms, it's not original to me but so applicable. If you have ever flown on a commercial jet you have heard the stewardess say, "Please put your own mask on, then assist those in need around you." Why do you think they say this? They know that if you put masks on your children first and then pass out because of a lack of oxygen, the first thing your children will do is take off their mask. Everyone is in danger.

This incredible task the Lord has given to us will demand time and attention. It doesn't just happen! Praise the Lord for Sunday school teachers, Christian schoolteachers and Godly grandparents in our children's lives that help us. But it is not their responsibility to meet this need in our homes. God has called us as mothers to this very fruitful task.

As godly mothers, our children do not get in the way... raising our children, for us, IS THE WAY! It is God's calling in our lives! Have you embraced this calling?

A little Homework...

A. *Begin praying for your children/grandchildren every day and for wisdom for yourself as you deal with them. *List 3 things to pray for concerning them and their future.*

B. *List four different goals you have for your children when they are adults.*

C. What are some of the steps you can take <u>now</u> to get them there?

D. Get a notebook and begin taking notes during preaching and Bible lessons this month. Look for at least one thing you can put in your life for each service.

E. Write the definition for diligent down.

F. Build a pyramid this week with a line dividing the important and optional. Plan to accomplish the important tasks and work in a few optional ones.

G. Name at least three changes you can start implementing in your home daily this month. At the end of the month write the benefits these changes made.

H. Does God have a ministry for you, but you are too busy to assume it? (or) Are you so deep in ministry and responsibilities that you are not the sentry in your children's lives you should be? There is a balance.

Memory Verse

Deuteronomy 11:18*...Therefore shall ye lay up these my words in your heart and in your soul, and bind them for a sign upon your hand, that they may be as frontlets between your eyes.*

Glorious Within Her Heritage

Chapter Ten

Our first Purpose: Organization

Mothering has many hats to wear. Most tasks aren't pretty, and seldom will anyone fight you for them. They are often overlooked unless you are not there to do them. During our many years on the road, living in an RV, my children sang and played instruments before my husband's preaching. We also taught Sunday school, children's ministries and did puppet shows. But it was not uncommon for me to hear from people, "What do you do?" As if all that just materialized.

If your desire is not to just survive parenting, but to put out a godly product, you are going to need a plan. The old saying, 'If you aim for nothing, you will be sure to hit it,' is true. My good all-around recipe for Mothering is 90 percent Organization, 90 percent Flexibility, with a dash of Creativity. Today we are going to look at the Organization part.

Organization: having one's affairs in order so as to deal with them efficiently.

Efficiently: An adverb. A way that achieves maximum productivity with minimum wasted effort or expense

Our Bible definition:

> *I Corinthians 14:40, Let all things be done decently and in order.*

This infers things need to be done. There is work to do! And done in an orderly and proper manner. Isaiah 32:9 says, 'Rise up, ye women that are at ease; hear my voice, ye careless daughters.' Raising godly children is not a 'fly by the seat of your pants' or 'wait and see what happens' kind of job. I love these descriptive words, 'efficiently and decently'. If we are going to do that kind of a job, we are going to have to stop and get organized.

You will need a Plan. Here are a few things I have found that have helped me raise my six children. They by no means are exhaustive, but maybe they can add some direction.

1. A Plan for <u>Discipline</u>.

> ***Proverbs 22:6...Train up a child in the way he should go: and when he is old, he will not depart from it.***

Sit down with your husband and make a list of offences and their consequences. The consequences need to become more severe after each offence. Some children are quick learners while others need more "encouragement". Having a list will help you not to lose your cool. Plus, you can show the child how their action brought about the punishment, not you. They already were aware of the expectations and consequences. Remember, you need to train your children on the appropriate behavior or task first, before you can have an expectation.

Training anything will take time and repetition. Here is a way that helped me. I identified a problem area and for an entire week I repeatedly trained with small consequences and warnings. It's good to use God's Word as an aid. Then during the second week I 'upped the ante'. Every time the rule was broken, I confronted the child with the rule and their offence and administered punishment. Nothing to talk about, no arguing and no mercy! The third week was harsher yet with additional penalties until I got the results I was looking for. An example of this would be that my children loved to go to the library. We would schedule to meet their friends there every week. If there was an attitude problem and a failure to obey, they would not be allowed to go to the library, thus, they would miss their friends and the opportunity to check out books, meaning they would only have to read whatever their siblings picked out. To take that privilege from them would immediately bring tears and a repentant heart. These consequences invariably brought about the desired results. Do not compromise and be swayed by tears. (you have nothing to apologize for) Be wise in your determination of consequences. For instance, I do not send the child to her room who loves to be by herself. There would be no profit from that punishment. There is always something they don't want to part with or do.

Some time ago a lady with four children came to me and said she had a terrible problem with complaining and whining in her home. She asked if I had any helpful advice. I told her, "You need to have a rule of no complaining and train your children about the consequences." She said, "We already have a rule." My response was rather simple, "There is no rule, or your children would not be complaining." They do what they are allowed to do." I saw her two years later and she proudly exclaimed, "You will find no complaining in our home! Thank you for your advice!" She went on to tell me that the benefits of keeping that rule helped them to keep others and they were enjoying being parents."

I want to show you a very sobering example of what happens when we do not train and discipline correctly.

I Samuel 2:22-24...Now Eli was very old, and heard all that his sons did unto all Israel; and how they lay with the women that assembled at the door of the tabernacle of the congregation. And he said unto them, why do ye such things? For I hear of your evil dealings

> *by all this people. Nay, my sons; for it is no good report that I hear: ye make the Lord's people to transgress.*

Eli was the chief priest at the time. He was to train his sons how to perform the many tasks of God's temple ministry and to represent holiness. In time one of them would replace him. God's desire was for His house to be a Holy place and that His people would come there to meet God and hear from Him.

Did you see the accusations the people made against Eli's sons? They complained about 'all their evil dealings'. It says by 'all' the people. Eli was aware of the problem. It sounds like it had been going on for some time. What they did was no secret. I am sure the people no longer viewed the temple or God's commands in a positive manner, nor thought of it as a Holy place. Eli's sons tore down the reputation of the Lord by their examples and dealings.

> ***I Samuel 3:13**...his sons made themselves vile, and he restrained them not.*

What God is saying is that Eli knew what his boys did but refused to get involved. There were no consequences for their actions. He was not training them. Because of Eli's disobedience he and his lineage suffered a self-induced curse.

> ***I Samuel 3:13-14**...For I have told him that I will judge his house for ever for the iniquity which he knoweth; because his sons made themselves vile, and he restrained them not. And therefore, I have sworn unto the house of Eli, that the iniquity of Eli's house shall not be purged with sacrifice nor offering for ever.*

What an awful thing to do to your own children and grandchildren. Is there something you are ignoring that is going to bring about a curse in your family?

> ***Proverbs 22:15***...*Foolishness is bound in the heart of a child; but the rod of correction shall drive it far from him.*
>
> ***Proverbs 23:13,14***...*Withhold not correction from the child: for if thou beatest him with the rod, he shall not die. Thou shalt beat him with the rod, and shalt deliver his soul from hell.*

2. You need a plan for <u>Order</u>.

> <u>A plan for meals, naps and bedtimes</u>. Children need their sleep, and we need a little time to regroup. Even if they don't fall asleep, quiet time is good for everyone.

I have often heard a mom drop off her little ones at nursery and say, "We were busy, and they didn't get a nap or dinner. Here is a hamburger and fries for them. Hope they aren't too cranky for you." This is so wrong! You are the mom. These needs are yours to see that they get met. The nursery is there to assist you. It frees you up to hear the teaching of God's Word, not escape from your responsibilities. Our nursery workers deserve better and so do our children.

<u>A plan for manners</u>. What expectations are you going to have around the dinner table? How are they to address adults? How are they to act in public? You are always being watched. Do you cause people to want what you have by the way your children act?

<u>A plan for play and fun</u>. (interacting with others) Are you going to have overnights with friends? What about neighborhood play time, youth group outings, or dating? We are constantly reproving our children. Try to spend a little time each day playing and building your relationship with them. Encourage togetherness with every member of the family. We love to share the illustration," I'm not sure if God gave you your friends, but I can guarantee that He gave you your family members." So, treat them like the gift they are from God and train your children to do so, also.

<u>A plan for chores</u>. Will you have allowances? Everyone was responsible to clean their rooms and have them checked after breakfast. We set the standard for what was clean. I scheduled household chore time in the afternoon before dad would come home. I arranged chores on a weekly routine. I was always buzzing around helping the little ones learn and work and assisting others. (Remember that while one is learning you might have to settle for a little less quality.) We had lots of company and I had little outside help. I trained my children to watch the baby, to take coats, fill half cups of coffee, clear the table, take orders for dessert and serve. Their reward? They got to serve themselves an adult size dessert. Everyone was happy! Looking back now I realize I could not have done my ministry without my children's help. So, train them and work together for the Lord!

<u>A plan for friends</u>. In this day of social communication, you need to check, and keep checking, your children's friends in the movies they watch, games they play, music, phones and peers. Please be careful to note that simply because someone goes to church with you, does not mean they have the same convictions and standards.

> *I Corinthians 15:3... Be not deceived, evil communications (the socialization trap) corrupt good manners.*
>
> *Proverbs 13:20...He that walketh with wise men shall be wise: but a companion of fools shall be destroyed.*

I came up with a little saying that helped me identify friendships. As long as we are influencing them, the relationship is good! But when they began to influence us, the friendship is over. Our children make most of their decisions on how they enjoy something, not is it right or good for me. Friendships are no different. Spend time with them and their friends. Watch for the direction a friendship is going. You won't regret it.

3. A plan for <u>Education.</u>

> *Galatians 4:2...under tutors and governors until the time appointed of the father.*

The weighty decision of education and all its facets has been given by God to each father. The mother is quite often included in this process, but the final say is still dad. Where do the children attend school? Will they take piano lessons? Will there be after school sports, trade school or college? These are major decisions that affect the rest of our children's lives. Take the time to help them be prepared for the adult life and their service to the Lord. Help them choose a line of work that is suited to them and is needed in the work force.

4. A plan for <u>Service to God</u>

> *Joshua 24:15...Choose you this day whom ye will serve; but as for me and my house, we will serve the Lord.*

Service to God is an attitude...What kind of attitude do your children see when you are serving or are needed to serve? Doing the normal tasks at church is one thing. They are our duties. But what happens when that sick call comes in, or a need arises that requires your involvement? Like watching three 'not so well-behaved kids' for a weekend while their newly saved mom goes to see her dad before he passes away. At that moment they get that inside look at your heart. Does it have a, "Do I have too!" or" Do I get too!" attitude?

There are so many ways for our kids to serve in the house of God. Some ways our children can minister would include singing and visiting rest homes and shut-ins, aiding elderly and new mothers both before and after church, carrying umbrellas, making baked goods to give away, going on visitation, taking the offering, being greeters and cleaning up after fellowships, to name a few.

Things you can do at home...Family Bible memorization is a good one. Pick a chapter and quote a few verses at mealtimes and bedtime. Also set up a routine for praying for your missionaries at mealtimes or devotions. (I found it helpful to use their prayer cards, so the little ones could identify them.) Have your children adopt a missionary family and write to them and pray for them daily. Also, they can sing a special, quote a verse, or do a short Bible skit together. Have conversations about what they learned at church services and from the preaching. And be sure that when they are old enough, have them take notes. There is so much you can do to plant the seeds of service in their hearts.

5. A plan for your <u>Marriage</u>.

How are **you and your husband** doing? Some of the busiest years are when your children are young. Be sure you organize time for you and your husband. Find another young family and trade off watching each other's kids once a month for a date night. We would get together with several other couples for finger food and play games at one another's homes. In this age of electronics, text your man a sweet love note or thank you for doing something. Not just a request for bread or milk. Keep the honey in your marriage.

Boy! That looked like it would be such an easy lesson. How did we end up with so much on our plates? Let's get Organized!

A little Homework...

A. Write down the definition for organization and efficiency.

B. Make a list of offenses and the consequences. Pick the two most important, (write them down) chart an attack and for the next three weeks 'go to war.'

C. Write down one bad habit you wish to eliminate and one good habit you want to instill in each of your children's lives. Now make a three-step plan to see it happen this month.

D. How would your children grade your attitude towards serving the Lord and the unexpected needs that come into your life?

    a. Angry and hateful
    b. Ignore
    c. Dutiful and obligatory
    d. Respectful
    e. Loving and delightful

E. Does the order of your day meet the needs of your children? If you could tweak it, what two things would you do differently?

F. Incorporate at least a half hour fun time with your children every day.

G. Make a chore chart and train your children on what and how each is to be done.

H. Find a ministry that you can train your children to do and get involved in, as a family.

I. Is there something your children are known for that is tearing down the Lord or your testimony? (it can be an attitude or behavior)

J. Do people see your children, and their behavior, and give you a compliment? Would they, if they are still parents, want what you have?

Memory Verse

Deuteronomy 11:19... *And ye shall teach them your children, speaking of them when thou sittest in thine house, and when thou walkest by the way, when thou liest down, and when thou risest up.*

Glorious Within Her Heritage

Chapter Eleven

Our Second Purpose: Flexibility

We are looking at the gift of our children and grandchildren. How can we become more 'glorious' in our relationship with these very tender and easily influenced people in our lives? We were discussing my recipe for survival. 90 percent Organization, 90 percent Flexibility, with a dash of Creativity. Last time we went home with lots of homework and a startling reality of some things we weren't quite aware were our responsibility. Looking back, can you see some new organization habits that you have put in place that have helped your life run a little smoother?

Our second purpose is to invest 'Flexibility' in our heritage. It is a verb, and in school we learned that verbs are action words, meaning that some change is necessary. It requires some sort of task or doing.

Flexibility: ready and able to change to adapt to different circumstances.

When our oldest son turned 12 his request for his birthday was to watch Star Wars. His friends had been talking about it and everybody had light sabers. In our home we limited our TV to video only and used it very sparingly. Sci-fi was not on our list. However, we asked him to give us a day or two and we would get back to him. After some consideration, my husband and I decided that we would grant his request and sit down as a family and watch it together. We did not want him sneaking off to watch it and hoped this would keep communication open. It gave us lots to talk about without violating our end goal as parents.

Are you managing the circumstances with those you are responsible for? Do you know when to bend and what battles to fight? This only becomes tougher when we see those teenage years approaching. On one hand they can take care of many personal tasks and some around the house. But soon they begin to make judgment calls and want to start running things. The battle to want to grow up but not able to assume the responsibilities of those adult choices that every young person goes through is upon us.

It is not long into marriage that God blesses us with that little bundle of joy. We are so excited! Our life revolves around picking names, colors, themes, and morning sickness. Can any of you relate? We make plans to make all the baby food, no sugar, or preservatives for my baby! We research the car seats and whether to have bumper pads or not. Life is good! We think, like our teenagers, that we have everything under control. But that is because the baby is not here. The real responsibility of being a mom has not dawned yet.

Children bring about messes, noise, accidents, questions, and a lot of work. If that's not bad enough, they come to a point where they want to do everything themselves. 'I can do it!' they repeat so often. What we thought couldn't get any worse, does. We function on little sleep and little adult conversation. To top it off our husband asks the million-dollar question, 'What did you do today, Hon?'

Life is full of changes and these changes happen no matter what we do. We just need to expect them, so they don't conquer us. My daughter, who plays the piano, and son-in law, who plays the violin, have been asked to play for many weddings and different functions. Soon after Natalie was born, their first, they made plans to play for a wedding. My daughter found it difficult to practice and when the wedding came, she could hear her baby crying in the foyer. Although she had made sure Natalie was fed and all her needs met, she was not happy. More changes.

Isaiah 40:11...He shall feed his flock like a shepherd: he shall gather the lambs with his arm, and carry them in his bosom, and shall gently lead those that are with young.

This verse was a great comfort to me when I was a new mom. It is speaking of the Lord and his kind care for the flock. He takes great care of the young and the mothers. God did not have the same expectation for a mom with little ones as he does when they are all teenagers. In those early days I did not read my Bible through in a year. I did not even try. My prayer time was often interrupted and seldom finished in an organized manner. Most of the time it was a cry for help or 'are you sure I can handle more now Lord'. Now, I am an empty nester, no kids at home. I easily read my Bible in a year and have time to write this book that the Lord has laid on my heart. I read Bible study books and listen to preaching regularly. Life gets put on hold for a while when children are young, but it will return again.

A great example would be in Genesis 33 where Esau meats Jacob and volunteers to help move everyone along. Jacob says, "I will lead on softly...according as the children be able to endure."

We can only do so much if we are all going to make it in the end. The atmosphere will need to change and so will many dreams and expectations. Our husbands go out and do most of the heavy lifting in the workplace and we care for the children and many needs at home.

Here are a few guidelines that might help you navigate this rollercoaster of flexibility.

1. The principle of time. How much will this change squeeze your day? Can you regain any losses later or would letting one task slip by go unnoticed? Example: sports or extracurricular activities. All our events had to include the participation of most of my children and could not interfere with church. We did choir, orchestra, drama, unit study groups, archery, bowling and science lab, to name a few. (not all in one year). Example: A girl's home-economics group started, and my oldest two daughters wanted to attend. This required me driving twenty minutes one way twice every week. The teacher was a very godly woman, and the young ladies came from homes with similar goals. I made the sacrifice and enjoyed hearing and tasting the things they learned. This brings up...

2. Attitude. They came home with a sweeter attitude that more than made up for the loss of time on the road and the few chores that got set aside. In fact, they worked harder to help me in appreciation for taking them. Will this event you are contemplating putting your child in bring about a struggle with their attitude or way of thinking? We already have enough on our plate without piling more on.

3. The principle of resources. You need to discuss with your husband the importance for each extra activity and the finances it will chew up. Books, clothes, etc.

4. The principle of return. Will this activity help get your child to the end goal you have set for him/her? What battles or attitudes will it bring about? Arrogance, pride, independence, laziness, lack of faithfulness to the house of God or the things of God, unkindness to siblings, attitudes of rebellion, just to name a few?

Here are a few things that I put in place that helped to lighten the load.

1. **Learn to say No!**
    I didn't have extra time for in home parties. No trips to the mall. I made sure to keep our nap routine, and I turned the phone off from eight a.m. until after school at lunch. I spent a half hour or so sledding, taking a walk, kick ball or many other active things with my

kids in the afternoon. We all enjoyed this time and it was most important! Plan fun events. Make them fit your routine, the needs of your children and where you are in life.

2. **Get out your crock pot!**
    Find those recipes that appeal to your family and get cooking! What's nice is the liners you can get to put your meal in in the crock pot. When dinner is done, empty the leftovers, throw the bag away and rinse out the pot. Easy!

3. **Plan your menu and write your grocery list.**
    I made 2 or 3 larger meals a week setting portions aside to serve a few days later or made a casserole with the leftovers, thus cutting my prep time down incredibly.

4. **Make one shopping and errands day a week**
    I planned one day for all my running. Library, piano lessons, (We did school in the car while lessons were taking place), shopping, doctor visits, and occasionally a trip to McDonald's play place.

5. **Always have a snack and a change of clothes in the car for that accident.**

6. **Make a scheduled hourly chart for yourself.**
    Can you imagine what kind of shape your house would be in if you did a 20-minute job every hour? This was my basic schedule during those early days: After the baby's early morning feeding, around 6:30-7, I took my shower and began my day. This way I was able to get breakfast started before little feet were running around. Room check was after breakfast when I started the first of two loads of laundry that I did every day. School was from 8-12, (during this time the phone was off) lunch followed, with an hour of outside fun time for everyone. During the winter I saved spelling tests and any oral work for when I rode my stationary exercise bike. Then there was quiet time, followed by family chores. It was busy, but the

routine helped to keep things from falling through the cracks.

During our many years in Alaska we lived in a small nineteen hundred square foot home with up to nine of us. Life was busy and full of variety, but everyone wanted to come to our home. We look back and remember the volleyball after church on Sunday evenings. One orange igloo of water on the porch and everybody brought finger food. Thanksgiving was games and finger food from four to ten, ending in testimonies and songs. Every other Thursday we hosted a unit study with twelve to twenty children of all ages and their moms. Bible studies on Friday nights and company every Sunday. We had a busy little household, full of serving and play. This could not have happened without our schedule and being flexible.

Then there is life with teenagers. Mark Twain once said, "When you have children and they start becoming difficult, put them in a barrel with a hole. Feed them through the hole, but when they become teenagers, plug the hole."

Oh, the drama of still being a child, but wanting to be an adult without responsibility or experience. They hear from us how to behave and handle a situation and consider it their job to straighten things out. Including us. They see the inconsistency in what we do and how we act, and make a judgment without ever feeling the pressures or knowing all the information. Then they begin to resent our control in their life, thinking they can do a better job. Obviously, we are trying to keep them from enjoying what they want to do.

The best thing you can do during these years is 'engage, engage and engage again.' They need you so much more in their life now than they even know. Plan to do things together. Talk.

> ***Proverbs 23:26...****My son, give me thine heart, and let thine eyes observe my ways.*

What a verse to have in our arsenal as a mom. 'Give me your heart!' we shout. Everything would be so much more pleasant if we could put in what we wanted and have them chase the desires we think are best for them. One problem, we tend to concentrate on the first part of that verse and forget that they are watching us and what we do, and they don't want any part of it. Why? For two reasons. Number 1...They don't just see the choices we make and where they lead. They feel and endure them silently. Number 2...They see the inconsistencies and double standards that we have in our private life. We want them to give us their heart, but we are unwilling to live in such a way that it glorifies God in **every** area of our lives.

I notice that this verse is a request. I see a parent pleading and begging his son to give him a chance. 'You see the way I live and the things I chase. There is nothing more rewarding and fulfilling than serving my God. Won't you choose Him?' I also see a command given with confidence, 'Give me your heart, you have watched my faithfulness to the Lord and all that He has given me. I will use the same character and sacrifice to make you the very best you can be. You are my priority.'

> ***I Corinthians 11:1**, Be ye followers of me, even as I also am of Christ.*

God blessed me with a wonderful, godly Pastor during my high school years. Unfortunately, he passed away from a heart attack before we were ready to see him go. During the funeral each of his four children gave testimony to their dad. His youngest son said, "My dad was as real on a Monday as he was on a Sunday. I cannot remember one time where I saw him loose his temper, get short with one of us or walk in the flesh. I can't say one bad thing about my dad." Wow! What a testimony. I don't know about you, but my children can't say that about me. As I look back there are regrets. But I am not giving up! My goal now is to finish strong. Chasing my God and influencing my children and grandchildren in every way possible. Make your goal now to finish strong.

> ***Philippians 3:13**...Forgetting those things which are behind, and reaching forth unto those things which are before, I press toward the mark for the prize of the high calling of God in Christ Jesus.*

Here is a list that I have gathered through the years from several sources to help with those teenage years:

1. Keep talking to them. Learn to listen and get interested in things they enjoy. This is a must!
2. Make sure they know you love them. Don't just tell them, prove it.
3. Build Godly values in their lives: camps, missionary trips, revivals...
4. Have consequences for sin...that increases after each offense. Using God's word to define right and wrong and show them where that decision or sin will lead.
5. Build their self-esteem. Be truthful.
6. Challenge them with adult responsibilities.
7. Pray for them and point them to God.
8. Provide other Godly influences in their lives.
9. Give them an example of faithfulness to God to follow. These are difficult times whether you have little children or teenagers. Let those times drive you to God. He has the answers.

A little Homework...

    A. *Write down the definition of flexible.*

    B. *What is something that is not necessary in your life that you need to say, 'No!' to?*

C. If you are not writing a menu and shopping list, give it a try this month.

D. Start recording what you do with your time and how long a task takes. See if you can prioritize the important tasks and cut back on the time wasters of the day.

E. Try setting an hourly schedule. The first week or so things will move around. I set one chore for each hour leaving room for the many interruptions and unexpected demands of the day.

F. Looking at that list for teens, pick out one and start to incorporate it in your home.

G. Make your goals now so that you can finish strong.

   1. Write down 3 things that are hindering you from reaching your goal.

   2. What can be done in their place to get the desired results?

Memory Verse

Deuteronomy 11:20...*And thou shalt write them upon the door posts of thine house, and upon thy gates.*

Glorious Within Her Heritage

Chapter Twelve

Our Third Purpose: Creativity

This is my favorite! After looking at Organization and having to totally revamp our comfort zones and lives, then stumbling through the world of Flexibility, where there are no set rules, it's time for some Fun! Creativity! Adding color to everyone's lives but still maintaining your structure. At first glance you think it's impossible for these two to work together without destroying each other. That's not true. They work hand in hand to help each other grow, which in the long run stimulates your home and those in it to prosper.

creativity: a noun, the use of the imagination.
create: a verb, to do something constructive.

Everyone wants to feel like they are a part of something bigger than them. They want to be necessary and vital to its continuation. They are looking for something that is successful and exciting. They really don't mind the work. They just want to feel like they are important to a plan that is prosperous.' Not my kids!' you say. Look closely at their activities, when they are little, they are always looking for your approval upon what they created and want to help with whatever you are doing. It's not too long and sports becomes a big deal, Wow! if that is not group cohesion, I don't know what is. They are always clamoring to be with their friends and doing things with them. They make plans to have fun; who will come, what they will do, what they will eat and even what they will wear. They don't shy away from the tasks they need to do to make it all come together. God has given them the strong desire to form friendships. Their family should be the first one on that list.

> ***Proverbs 24:3,4...** Through wisdom is an house builded; and by understanding it is established: And by knowledge shall the chambers be filled with all precious and pleasant riches.*

We need both wisdom and understanding to build and establish our homes. Letting things 'fall where they may' will not lead to a happy ending. We are going to have to study to find out how God wants us to order our homes, so that we can have a godly and profitable result. That's what knowledge is. Learning what to do and observing your home, then figuring out the best way to go about it, is crucial. Is the energy of your home contagious? By the way, our children are some of those precious and pleasant riches.

Creativity has many mediums and can be perceived differently. Here are some of the things I thought of when my children were young.

The first thing I realized as a mom of six small children was that I had to figure out a way to include them in what I was already doing. I established a chore time that we referred to as 'Cinderella Time'. Everybody's participation was required. Individual chores were listed for the week and they knew what the end results were supposed to look like. This wasn't a grudging event. Because I had a cheerful attitude toward the many tasks that I was responsible for, my energy and joy was passed down to them. They didn't do the work themselves. I joined in and helped them, training and assisting where I was needed. Sometimes I had to exercise some flexibility and settle for less than perfect while they were learning. Majoring on their attitude and the effort to accomplish their job, we were working together to provide a clean atmosphere for us to live in.

When grocery shopping, I would go through the ads and cut out things I wanted to purchase. Each child was given the age-appropriate pictures to look for while we were in the store. If need be, I would write down how many and what kind. At the end of gathering all the groceries a free cookie awaited the well behaved and helpful children. Only the well behaved and helpful. I did not get talked into compromising! Whining and complaining had a very strong reward also.

My daughter-in-law parks by the grocery cart return so as not to have to leave the children or carry a car seat far.

Long drives can be tiresome and to a three-year-old 20 minutes is a long drive. During several years of our ministry, we had a 30-minute ride to church. What a good time to read to your children. Little House on the Prairie, Sugar Creek Gang and Heroes of the Faith series were just some of the many we read. It wasn't uncommon for dad to stop for fuel and request for us to wait till he returned, to hear the next chapter. It was fun for everyone, and the miles flew by painlessly.

At the end of quiet time Odyssey and Your Story Hour came on for an hour. It made for a happy wake up time as no grumpy faces were allowed. We folded laundry and I did the family ironing...two birds with one stone.

To cut down on glasses to wash, everyone had their own color or designed cup. They were responsible to rinse them during the day. After supper they were put into the dishwasher.

Make it a point to include your children. You will probably be impressed by what they can do. Train them along the way and settle for 'less than perfect' while they are learning. Figure a way to make the normal and mundane fun.

A Mother's Prayer

"Lord, give me patience when wee hands tug at me with their demands.
Give me gentle and smiling eyes; keep my lips from hasty replies.
Let not weariness, or noise, obscure my vision of life's fleeting joys.
So when, in years to come, my house is still; no bitter memories it's rooms may fill."

A little Homework...

A. How often do you incorporate Bible stories and spiritual conversation into your children's' lives?
   1. Never
   2. Rarely
   3. Sometimes
   4. Frequently
   5. Consistently

B. How would your children describe your attitude and tone of communication towards them?
   1. Angry and hateful
   2. Ignore and tolerate
   3. Dutiful and obligatory
   4. Respectful
   5. Loving and delightful

C. If your children were to describe you as a Bible character, who would they choose?
   1. Jezebel...
       * Rebellious
       * Self-willed
       * Destructive.
   2. Rebekah...
       * Complaining
       * Never content
       * Deceitful.
   3. Sapphira...
       * Focused on self.
       * Not influencing future generations in a positive way.
   4. Martha...
       * Worker
       * Busy in good things, but little spiritual fruit.
       * Focus is outside the home.
   5. Rahab...
       * Former life of sin.

* Thankful for forgiveness.
* Influences future generations positively.
6. Hannah...
   * Consistent and faithful.
   * Prayer warrior.
   * Continually looking towards her family's needs.
7. Ruth...
   * Loyal and sacrificial, though under great opposition.
   * Impacted future generations positively.

D. What is one habit or attitude you have toward your children that is destructive?

*What consequence or damage has occurred because of this habit?

*List at least two steps that you can take to change this area of your life.

Memory Verse

***Deuteronomy 11:21...** That your days may be multiplied, and the days of your children, in the land which the LORD sware unto your fathers to give them, as the days of heaven upon the earth.*

Glorious Within Her Heritage

After-Action Report

The years while your children are young and very busy, are some of the most trying times of a mom's life. Keeping order, nurturing little minds, providing for endless needs while maintaining sanity is no easy task. Little sleep and few breaks can wear one down. Many days it's like taking two steps forward and one step back. Can you relate? Then we graduate to raising a teenager. The hugs, smiles and silliness disappear, we wake up to someone who is hard to please, moody and often challenging our every decision. Yet God promises to bless if we are faithful to this task.

I hope that you were able to find some help and direction to apply in this stage of life. Let's look back at some of the nuggets we gleaned. Again, I encourage you to get some paper and go over the questions and your answers from the lessons in this section. Re-read and see if you missed something. 'Feedback is the breakfast of champions', and we need all the help we can get.

A little homework...

A. Are you happy with your hourly schedule? If not, work on finding one that helps lighten your workload but meets the needs of your family.

B. Write the definitions for organized and flexible down.

* Try writing the opposite of 'organized' and 'flexible' down and see if that sheds a little extra light on the subject.

C. List a couple of the organizational habits you put into practice and what benefits you are enjoying now?

D. What would be another organizational habit you would like to implement?

    * List two changes you can do to make this habit yours.

E. What do your children's 'friends' look like? (movies, video games, people, books, social media, music, etc....)

F. List two things you can do to see better results in the education of your children?

G. What ministry have you added as a family and how has it impacted others and your family?

    * How can you improve it?

H. Is there an event your children are involved in that is bringing about a wrong attitude?

I. What is hindering you from finishing strong?

* List two things you can do to ensure that you will finish strong.

J. List two creative things you have implemented into your home this last month?

* What positive return are you enjoying from them?

Here is a quick review of our 'Attack Program' for training children.
1. Find one area or habit.

2. Organize a training time.
   a. teach them what, how, and when to do it.
   b. explain the consequences.

3. Do it faithfully and cheerfully with them. Remember we are training them to be self-controlled, so we need to be the example.

4. After assisting them for a few times, let them do it by themselves. Inspect, compliment, and instruct.
   a. set a timer and check on them.
   b. reward good and bad behavior.

5. Stay with it for a few weeks.

A man came home from work and found his three children outside, still in their pajamas, playing in the mud with empty food boxes and wrappers strewn all around the front yard. The door of his wife's car was open, as was the front door to the house and there was no sign of the dog. Proceeding into the entry, he found an even bigger mess. A lamp had been knocked over, and the throw rug was wadded against one wall. On the front room the TV was loudly blaring a cartoon channel and the family room was strewn with toys and various items of clothing.

In the kitchen, dishes filled the sink, breakfast food was spilled on the counter, the fridge door was open wide, dog food was spilled on the floor, a broken glass lay under the table, and a small pile of sand was spread by the back door. He quickly headed up the stairs, stepping over toys and more piles of clothes, looking for his wife. He was worried she might be ill, or that something serious had happened. He was met with a small trickle of water as it made its way out the bathroom door. As he rushed to the bedroom. he found his wife still curled up in the bed in her pajamas, reading a novel. She looked up at him, smiled, and asked how his day went? He looked at her bewildered and asked: "What happened here today?"

She again smiled and answered, you know every day when you ask me what in the world I do all day? "Yes", was his incredulous reply.

She answered, "Well, today I didn't do it."

*Kellymom.com

review Deuteronomy 11:18-21

Part Four

Glorious In Her Habits

Glorious in Her Habits

Chapter Thirteen

Glorious in Her Habits

We have invested sixteen lessons looking at this 'Glorious' daughter. We started with her Heart, which led us to her happiness, her love life and her Husband. Lastly, we looked at her precious treasures, her Heritage. The children and grandchildren God has so richly blessed her with. How she is faithful to train, protect and influence them during those very tender and moldable years. She is truly a remarkable woman. The example each one of us is looking for to follow. If you were to analyze this 'Glorious' daughter and look for some defining markers, what would some of them be? Do you see them in your life and home?

These defining markers I encouraged you to look for in her life are called 'Habits.' We all have them. They are what makes us who we are. People know us by these in our lives and base their opinion of us on them. It is our reputation.

> habit: an established manner or practice
> reputation: overall quality or character as seen or judged by people in general

Habits are developed over time by training or consistent repetition. In the end, you do not think about them, you just do them. It is said that it takes approximately thirty days to make or change a habit. God desires us to develop good and godly habits. This will take effort and energy. Many times, we do not think why we do or think a certain way. We have never asked if it is good or godly. We just do it like we always have and live with the consequences. The habits of those around us or what is commonly accepted by them, makes some questionable habits acceptable. The idea, 'Everyone is doing it!' rules. They don't seem to be suffering any harm and some of them are Christians. We don't want to miss out on what looks like fun and seems harmless. Besides, as far as we can see, in and of itself, it is not hurting anything.

We need to challenge these ideas and habits in our lives. Could we be participating in something that in the end will bring about a regret or casualty? Are there habits that are slowly destroying us and those around us? Could it be that one day we will turn around and be cut down by what we thought was harmless? This is very sobering and will require some thought and concentration if we are to see victory in our habits.

> *Romans 12:21...Be not overcome of evil, but overcome evil with good.*

God is saying that the good in our life will overcome the evil that comes our way. The trick is, the good just doesn't appear. We don't wake up and find a good habit. On the contrary, we tend to fall into the evil habits easily. Many people take the path of least resistance and good habits usually require some thought and training. You have to say 'No' to what is natural many times and persevere in what is good. We are required to have good things being practiced in our lives. How do we keep from getting bitter or angry? We must change the habits of thinking we have lived with for so long. How do we live the Christian life? We must change the habits of what we immerse ourselves in. How are we to be ready to answer the call to service? By new habits of cleanliness, organization and compassion being practiced. As you can see our habits enable us or cripple us.

I have 11 grandchildren and they do some funny things that make my husband and I laugh. Recently during the Christmas season two of our grandchildren did a special for us. Our five-year-old granddaughter played the piano while our three-year-old grandson sang, 'Joy to the World.' Natalie played a resemblance of the song we enjoy during this time of year while Zachary sang at the top of his lungs. Though the words were utterly indistinguishable their enthusiasm made us laugh uncontrollably. We expect them to do those things. They are young. But we would not be laughing if they continued to do them, later in life. We expect the words and notes to be learned. Their parents are responsible to teach them habits that will help them be responsible adults.

> *I Corinthians 13:11...When I was a child, I spake as a child, I understood as a child, I thought as a child; but when I became a man, I put away childish things.*

Just like a child, there are many things we discontinue doing as we grow and mature. We learn that some habits are offensive or just not as much fun as they use to be. Something is just not quite right if a 30-year-old is known for sucking their thumb. Spiritually we also begin to grow and slowly adapt habits of a mature Christian. Instead of just reading devotionals we start a daily Bible reading time where we study ourselves. We put off immature habits and began to be faithful to church, giving, growing in the fruit of the Spirit, having victory over sin, reading missionary and other Christian literature, teaching a class and participating in the services. All of these become our new reputation. We get excited about missions and take an active part in sharing with others what we have received. Sooner or later we experience the great joy of leading someone to Christ. These are steps of growth in our spiritual life.

> *I Corinthians 3:12,13...Now if any man build upon this foundation gold, silver, precious stones, wood, hay, stubble; Every man's work shall be made manifest: for the day shall declare it, because it shall be revealed by*

> *fire; and the fire shall try every man's work of what sort it is.*

Every man's work could also represent our personal habits. Like bitterness, hate, apathy, and pride. God is always watching his children and he has expectations for each of us. But he is not a grandpa! He wants us to grow and become a tool that He can use to bring himself glory. If we are careless and allow our evil habits to rule, the wood, hay and stubble will burn, and we will be left with nothing. If you are living a secret life of sin, God says that it will be made known. He sees it all. God will not allow us to be one thing on a Sunday and something else on a Monday. No one shall escape from this day of accountability.

On a good note, if we are faithful to build habits that are godly, the gold, silver and precious stones will pass the test of time and fire. Qualities such as forgiveness, confession of sin, peace and joy. These jewels will help protect us from the many bad things that would come into our life and try to destroy us. In the end, they will bring the Lord glory and give us a reason to rejoice and praise him. Not that we won't experience hard times in this life, but we have the Lord to walk with us as we go through them.

> *II Peter 3:11…what manner of persons ought ye to be in all holy conversation and godliness?*

This is a question. What is your conversation and life reflecting? It should be our heavenly Father and his desires. God wants us to analyze what we are doing? Could you say that every word you speak is holy and has the Lord's blessing upon it? By the way you live and act would people in your community say you are a God-fearing lady? Our good habits are there to protect us. They are what we do automatically. It is what we do when we confront any situation in our lives. It is second nature to us. There are times in our lives when we are minding our own business, happily serving, when around the corner we hear something not meant for our ears. What you do and think in those situations is who you are. We have all been there. Looking back, did your response look holy or godly to you?

> ***Psalms 101:2...I will behave myself wisely in a perfect way. I will walk within my house with a perfect heart.***

I love how this verse comes across. It seems to say that you can count on me, 'I will behave myself in a godly manner!' Whether in private or public I will do what is right. Is your testimony so strong that if a rumor was started people would say, "No way!" She would never do or be a part of something like that! Further, it mentions our walk at home or what we do in private. A 'perfect' heart has the idea that there is nothing between you and the Savior. Our actions at home should be drawing the ones we love closer to God. They get to see us in our private lives and habits. What would your children say? Would they testify that your walk with God, how you lived and your personal habits drew them into a closer relationship with Him?

Our reputation is developed by our habits, both good and bad.

> Watch your thoughts, they become words.
> Watch your words, they become your actions.
> Watch your actions, they become habits.
> Watch your habits, they become your character.
> Watch your character, it becomes your Destiny.

This would be a good time to lift your heart in prayer to God asking for direction and insight. Changing a lifetime of habits is no easy task but living with ungodly or questionable ones is even worse. The list of broken lives and regrets are endless. The next series of lessons will help us to identify more in-depth habits. We need to have our bad habits pointed out. Many times, we are in denial and are not repentant, thus we see no need for correction. Plan to make concentrated prayer time in this area daily. If you spend little or no time, you will get little or no lasting fruit in producing good habits.

> *Psalm 139: 23,24...Search me, O God, and know my heart: try me and know my thoughts: and see if there be any wicked way in me, and lead me in the way everlasting.*

A little Homework...

1. Write down the definition for habits and reputation.

2. List 3 good habits in your life.

   * What blessings are you receiving because of each of them?

3. List 3 bad habits in your life.

   a. What damage have they caused?

   b. List 2 steps for each to change them into good habits.

4. List 10 habits that would be in a 'glorious' daughter's life.

5. Now, list 2 steps for each one that can be taken to make them a good or godly habit.

6. After seeing what it takes to make these habits yours, why not consider a few to implement into your life?

7. Carve some time out of your day and write out a prayer for you to use this week to help you see your habits the way the Lord does. Be willing to confront those bad habits and ask for guidance to implement new habits. Pray that prayer at least two times each day this week.

Memory verse

Psalm 101:2... *I will behave myself wisely in a perfect way. I will walk within my house with a perfect heart.*

Glorious in Her Habits

Chapter Fourteen

Our Private Habits of Negative Thinking

Spiritual growth and physical health start in our minds. What we think and meditate on can affect our moods and how we feel. God in his great wisdom created us as emotional beings. He wanted us to enjoy thinking about Him and all that he has done for us. He also wanted us to form strong bonds with those in our care so that we would be sensitive to their needs. Causing us to perceive the needs of those around us and plan to sacrifice to meet them. This is the positive use of our emotional thinking. It is focused on others and how we can assist them. My children play the piano, and many times as they were growing up, I could sense a need in their life by the music they chose to play. The anger or hurt they were feeling came through, warning me that I needed to set time aside to help my young person through something they were struggling with. Are you using this incredible gift of perception for those around you?

Unfortunately, like so many other things the Lord meant to strengthen us, we take our habit of thinking and make it all about us. It is not uncommon for us to take something minor, put it into our thought processing machine and before long we have built a case on what we thought was meant by the words or actions around us. This is very destructive! Negative habits of thinking can only bring about negative habits of feeling.

> ***Pro 23:7a...****For as a man thinketh in his heart, so is he.*

Pride is a Habit of thinking that should not be in a 'glorious daughter's life.' It is a negative habit of thinking. Who or what do you trust? Many are trusting in themselves, what they have or what they have done or not done. We forget that all we have and enjoy came from the hand of our gracious Lord. He equips each one of us with different gifts, talents, and abilities. Not for us to achieve a higher position but to accomplish his will. Singing, the ability to teach, playing an instrument, keeping nursery, cleaning the church house, and making visits are each just as important as the other. There are no little you' s and big I's in the Lord's family. If we are not careful, we become puffed up with our abilities and begin to *think more highly than we ought to think, Romans 12:3*. We are all sinners saved by grace. There is no stepladder of success because of the better life you lived, the lack of certain sin in your life or the family you came from.

> ***Ps. 49:6...****They that trust in their wealth and boast themselves in the multitude of their riches.*
> ***Luke 18:9...****And he spake this parable unto certain which trusted in themselves that they were righteous, and despised others.*
> ***I Peter 5:5...****For God resisteth the proud and giveth grace to the humble.*
> ***James 3:14...****But if ye have bitter envying and strife in your hearts, glory not, and lie not against the truth.*

Many are dealing with the Habit of fear. Life can seem so frightening at times. Some of you dear ladies have been physically or sexually abused, not loved and taken care of. These things are real and should in no wise be ignored. In this day of outward focus, you might feel inadequate and self-conscious. Many times, the circumstances of life can be overwhelming. Sickness, loss of a loved one or job, a rebellious child, lost spouse and sin are just a few. Thankfully, we do not have to go through these things on our own. Your heavenly Father is there with you and he has provided a church family to support you.

> **Psalm 121**...*My help cometh from the Lord.*
> **Galatians 6:2**...*Bear ye one another's burdens, and so fulfil the law of Christ.*

While some of these fearful thoughts come from genuine circumstances and need addressed, some of us think and create an imaginary fear in our minds that control how we think and respond, making life miserable for all. Have you heard the term, 'hypochondriac?' defined as one with an obsession with the idea of having a serious medical condition. We live in fear and miss out on so much. Some see life as a cup half full, while others see it half empty. What kind of person are you? Are you operating like something bad has already happened or going to happen?

> **II Timothy 1:7**...*For God hath not given us the spirit of fear; but of power, and of love, and of a sound mind.*
> **Proverbs 29:25**...*The fear of man bringeth a snare: but whoso putteth his trust in the Lord shall be saved.*

> ***Matt. 8:26**...And he saith into them, Why are ye fearful, O ye of little faith? Then he arose, and rebuked the winds and the sea; and there was a great calm,*
> ***Isaiah 26:3**...Thou wilt keep him in perfect peace, whose mind is stayed on thee: because he trusteth in thee.*

Another very negative habit of thinking is 'bitterness.' This is a wide-spread epidemic in our lives. We seem to find some pleasure in playing the victim and continually reliving those moments. Holding someone's feet to the fire 'till we feel like they have paid the appropriate price. We claim innocence to any involvement in whatever the event was. Always bringing it up and never letting it go, even if the party apologized.

> ***Hebrews 12:15**...Looking diligently lest any man fail of the grace of God; lest any root of bitterness springing up trouble you, and thereby many be defiled.*
> ***Psalm 119:165**...Great peace have they which love thy law: and nothing shall offend them.*
> ***Ephesians 4:31**...Let all bitterness...be put away from you.*

This brings up that topic of selfishness. It is an all-consuming negative habit in so many of our lives and we give it free reign. I believe it is the root problem behind ALL our negative habits of thinking. Our first habit of thought tends to be inward. How will this affect ME! Because of this, 'Bad' habit of selfishness, we have difficulty letting things go. I personally have to work on forgetting misunderstandings between my husband and me. He thinks so differently and tends to work and make decisions without me in mind. If I don't consciously cast down these thoughts, I will stop enjoying the great things we have together and will miss out on building happy memories now. Things tend to get bigger each time we think about them. Some are just not that important and we make a mountain out of a mole hill. Recently we were parked at an RV park. I was outside doing my devotions and a lady next door was reading her husband the riot act. I was so embarrassed for him. Through the conversation I learned that one of their four children had left their shoe at the pool. The pool was within walking distance. Wow! What a storm for an insignificant shoe. We, so many times do the same thing with what happens in our daily lives. Shoes will get forgotten. It's not the shoe that's the problem but our selfish response.

These negative habits of thinking cultivate a spirit of anger and bitterness. We feel justified after the case we built in our minds on what we imagined happened. We begin to function like it is fact and our actions and words convey the anger and bitterness inside. Those around us feel threatened and confused as our actions don't line up with the truth. They, in turn, perceive our hostilities and respond in like manner if they aren't walking closely to the Lord. What a needless mess we have created! I am guilty of this, are you?

A little Homework...

1. *From 1-10, 10 being high, how much of your gift of perception are you using for others?*

2. *Write down 2 situations where you used your thought processing machine in a negative way this last week.*

3. *Would you say that your first thoughts to an unexpected situation are mostly negative or positive?*

4. *Name one thing in your life that can sneak up on you and can become a source of pride?*

5. Write some thank you notes for those in your life and church family to encourage them.
   a. Pray and thank the Lord for them.
   b. What are they doing that can challenge you?

6. Are you a 'half full' or 'half empty' kind of person? What 2 things can you do to be a consistent 'half full' kind of person?

7. List 3 things that bring about gloomy feelings in your thoughts?

8. List 2 things for each that you can do to make the sunshine more permanently.

Memory Verse

***II Corinthians 10:5...**Casting down imaginations, and every high thing that exalteth itself against the knowledge of God, and bringing into captivity every thought to the obedience of Christ.*

Glorious in Her Habits

Chapter Fifteen

Our Private Habits of Positive Thinking

Spiritual prosperity and success start in our mind and how we think and what we dwell on. In I Samuel 30 it says, *but David encouraged himself in the Lord his God.* God never intended for our feelings or what is going on around us to make our decisions. Our mind must choose what is right for us to think, and our will must enforce our thoughts and rule our emotions. How does a 'glorious daughter' smile and praise the Lord while going through trials? She has learned to encourage herself in the Lord and trust Him.

> **Romans 12:2**...*And be not conformed to this world: but be ye transformed by the renewing of your mind, that ye may prove what is that good, and acceptable, and perfect, will of God.*

This was a favorite verse of my Pastor's when I was a teen. I don't think he ever missed a chance to bring it to our attention. It does, however, use a few words that I would like to define for you.

conformed: to be, or become similar in form, nature or character.

transformed: to make a thorough or dramatic change in the form, appearance, or character of something.

renewed: to make like new, restore or refresh.

This verse is very clear that we are **not** to be like the world, even in our habits of thinking. Our Father wants us to transform or change from the world's habits and norms to His. Casting down those thoughts that are worldly and lifting one's self up.

He wants us to have thoughts that will be tried through our daily experiences and respond as He would, bringing Him glory. These thoughts will bring about *'that good and acceptable, and perfect, will of God.'* What kind of response do you have during the day? Your thoughts are revealed through them.

> **II Corinthians 10:5**...*Casting down imaginations, and every high thing that exalteth itself against the knowledge of God, and bringing into captivity every thought to the obedience of Christ.*

Let's look at the *'transforming and renewing'* that is supposed to happen. The definition says that a 'dramatic change' will take place. How does that sound to you? Painful? That's what I thought. It's amazing to see a butterfly and realize that such a beautiful creature came from a caterpillar. When we exercise godly thoughts, they are viewed by others through our actions and words. They do not see a worldly response or what we used to be before Christ. A dramatic change has taken place. No one would guess what we were before salvation. Does your life represent this dramatic change?

> **Philippians 2:5-8**...*Let this mind be in you, which was also in Christ Jesus: who...made himself of no reputation, and took upon him the form of a servant...and humbled himself.*
> **Romans 12:3**...*For I say, through the grace given unto me, to every man that is among you, not to think of himself more highly than he ought to think; but to think soberly, according as God hath dealt to every man the measure of faith.*

Humility seems to be a necessary ingredient if we are going to be 'glorious' in the 'Private Habits of our positive Thinking'. We never see our Lord justifying himself or arguing about who He is. He was willing to help and do anything. No need or people group was too low for him to stoop and help. This will not be a habit that we just pick up. We will have to train our minds and then put it into practice with our actions. Our Lord was a servant in his mind; thus, he was a servant in everything he did.

We expect a level of treatment. Have you ever thought, "How dare they say that to me! Don't they know who I am?" Well, that is not humility and it does not bring glory to our Father. We must come to the place where we have no will of our own. Willing to live righteously through any circumstance.

Here is a great verse to use to sift out your thoughts.

> ***Phil. 4:8...Finally brethren whatsoever things are true, whatsoever things are honest, whatsoever things are just, whatsoever things are pure, whatsoever things are lovely, whatsoever things are of good report; if there be any virtue, and if there be any praise, think on these things.***

What an inspirational verse! Just reading it makes one feel clean and free. Can you imagine how happy we would be if this was what we thought on daily? This is not an instant event, but a life-long pursuit. It is not perfection but direction. Christ empowers us to think differently and gives us a *'sound mind'*, ***II Timothy 1:7***. But like so many of the things that we find in this 'glorious daughter's life, it will take perseverance and time.

We need to take control of our thoughts and make them our servants. How can we attack these negative habits of thinking? You are going to need the help of your caring Father. Begin by asking for his help and forgiveness often. Like so many of our habits they didn't get there overnight, and it will take perseverance and time to remove them. Copy some of these verses and carry them with you so you can refer to them in a moment of weakness. If you are able, memorize them. Keep your awareness up and be ready to cast down any thoughts that do not follow Philippians 4:8 and replace them with godly thoughts. I strongly encourage you to have a thought journal where you record when and what negative thoughts you are having. Write down the positive thinking that you put in its place. This way you can address them immediately and change that habit into a good and blessed one. It is such a blessing when you see those bad thoughts come into your mind less frequently. Find someone to be accountable to that can ask you specifically how you are doing and pray for you.

Steps to Attack Negative Habits of Thinking

1. Daily and specifically ask your Father's help and forgiveness.
2. Copy verses down and refer to them during the day. Try to memorize them.
3. Immediately, acknowledge and cast down negative thoughts.
4. Confess and ask forgiveness.
5. Replace them with godly thoughts and prayers for those involved.

A little Homework…

1. Name a few trials you have or are going through. (don't leave out emotional or personal trials)

    a. Was your habit of thinking negative or positive?

    b. What specifically could you have done to change your thinking into positive thinking?

c. What type of actions will accompany positive thinking?

d. List one verse to add to your arsenal the next time a trial comes along.

2. Circle any habit of thinking you have that is patterned after the world? selfish, proud, complaining, pouting, bitter, angry, ...

3. What would be 3 ways you can transform your mind?

4. How are you hoping you will benefit from them?

5. List 2 ways you can add the attitude of humility to your life.

6. Start a 'Habit of Thinking' journal.

7. List the 8 positive habits of thinking in Philippians 4:8.
   * List a verse after each one.

Memory verse

Romans 12:2...*And be not conformed to this world: but be ye transformed by the renewing of your mind, that ye may prove what is that good, and acceptable, and perfect, will of God.*

Glorious in Her Habits

Chapter Sixteen

Our Public Habits

Our public habits are what everybody sees and experiences. It is the norm in our life. They are controlled by our Habits of thinking. Both negative and positive. They are the actions that accompany those thoughts. We have two places where we exercise these habits. At home and in public. It is very critical that the habits in these two places do not vary too much. That awful word, 'Hypocrite,' is not a title we want to have, but, if we are not practicing the same habits in both places it will become one of our defining markers. Let's define what a hypocrite is.

<u>hypocrite</u>: *A false appearance of virtue or goodness, while concealing real character and flaws.*

Most of the time we exhibit our best behavior and habits in the public eye, leaving our family members to live with a different person. I totally agree that it is hard to be your best all the time. If there is one place where I am more likely to be lax it will be at home. But we should strive to be the same person no matter where we are.

What would be a few of these ungodly habits that should not be in our life, at home or in public. I don't want to spend lots of time defining these negative habits, but we do need to mention them.

<u>Anger</u>. *harsh, unnecessary words or actions used to express our feelings.* Slamming doors, stomping around, angry words or the silent treatment. I've heard of some ladies going on a spending spree if they don't get their way. How many actions of anger do you exhibit every day?

> ***Proverbs 25:28**...He that hath no rule over his own spirit is like a city that is broken down, and without walls.*

Laziness. *averse or disinclined to work. Marginal activity or exertion.* It is said that '10 percent of the people do 90 percent of the work.' It's amazing to me how some people are comfortable watching and enjoying the hard work of others. And it's always the same group on both sides. Which group are you a part of? Do you find yourself always arriving a little late and when you get there is something left behind or not done? What does the state of your home say concerning your care for it?

> ***Isaiah 32:9**... Rise up, ye women that are at ease; hear my voice, ye careless daughters; give ear unto my speech.*
> ***32:11**...Tremble, ye women that are at ease; be troubled, ye careless ones:*

There are those who are <u>self-absorbed or OCD,</u> always the 'center of attention', making all the decisions. We refer to them as 'Queen Bees'. The world must revolve around them, or they make life miserable. Always having to have the last word. When you walk in a room you know where they are. Does that sound like a habit the 'glorious daughter' would have?

Pouting. *thrusting out your lower lip, expressing annoyance or displeasure, moody or silent.* This is so childish but is very prevalent in women. If we don't get our way, we sit in the corner and fuss like a 2-year-old.

Rebellion. *the action or process of resisting authority, control or rule.* Do you ever find yourself not happy with a decision your husband made, or being corrected by him? I do and it's not a pleasant feeling. What about the rules around you? Wearing seatbelts, using your smart phone while driving or speeding are easy tests to find out if you are rebellious. They are all regulated laws.

> *I Samuel 15:23...For rebellion is as the sin of witchcraft. and stubbornness is as iniquity and idolatry.*

Enough of that! Let's investigate those godly habits we want to strengthen and add to our lives. What would be at the top of your list? The police force motto, "Protect and Serve", Marine Corps motto, "Always Faithful", Alaska State Troopers, "Loyalty, Integrity, Courage" and last of all, our marriage vows, "For better for worse, in sickness in health, to love, cherish and obey." If we are going to become that 'glorious daughter of the King' don't you think we should live above all these mottos? On our own this would be impossible, but thankfully we aren't on our own.

> *Psalm 119:133...Order my steps in thy word: and let not any iniquity have dominion over me.*

The habit of Bible reading, and prayer will be your starting point. It is where your strength will come from. This is the backbone of a 'glorious' daughter's life. Do you have a Bible reading schedule that you are faithfully following? How is your prayer time?

Have you ever considered your spirit as a Habit? What attitude do you add to the room when you walk in? Is it joyful, uplifting and challenging others to good works? Or is it negative and divisive? My girlfriend Stephanie is a joyful person. You can't miss the energy she brings into the room. Incredibly ebullient and cheerful. A visit from her is always welcomed. That's the spirit I want to have, how about you?

> *Pro. 17:22...A merry heart doeth good like a medicine: but a broken spirit drieth the bones.*

The words that we choose to use are also habits. They bring life and death. Have you ever thought after you left a conversation, 'what did I leave behind?' Was it encouraging to the hearer? Did it please my Heavenly Father? As we travel across the country, we meet lots of people in a short time. It is very important to us that we influence them for the Lord, encouraging them. Even a hug sends a message of self-worth. Do your words resemble a warm hug?

> *Proverbs 16:24...Pleasant words are as an honeycomb, sweet to the soul and health to the bones.*

Another area we need to give some attention to is our actions. *'the process of doing something, an act'*. Have you ever taken the time to analyze your daily habits? There are so many 'actions of habit' that we practice every day without thinking about them. Most are helpful to expedite our daily routines of life. But have you ever thought you could invest the time more wisely? What is consuming those hours that are so priceless? Are you getting the best return from the energy and time spent?

> *I Corinthians 10:31...Whether therefore ye eat, or drink, or whatsoever ye do, do all to the glory of God.*
> *Ephesians 5:16...Redeeming the time, because the days are evil.*

The habit of reading is a good one to get into. Besides your Bible why don't you read a missionary or Christian help book. Every month I pick one to read and am so encouraged and helped by them. I know, you with young children, have little time right now with so many responsibilities. When my children were young, I would read missionary stories to them before bed. It built our faith, hearing about those before us who trusted our great God with insurmountable odds. Great conversations came from that well spent half hour. It also helped me to keep my perspective right.

Speaking about time...do you have a habit for starting your day? Our friend, the Proverbs 31 woman did. She realized that if she was going to get everything done, she had to get up early. Organizing the things that needed done before the children were up. This allowed her to be cheerful and meet their needs efficiently. What are the most important things you need to do? Are you getting them done? Do you realize that when and how you wake up often defines who you are?

How is your faithfulness to church? Are you in the habit of helping and meeting needs? Would you be a pillar in your church? If your kids ever ask if you're going to church, you have your answer. This is also a habit. Faithfulness and service are both in a 'glorious daughters' life.

What about the habit of eating dinner together as a family? Life is terribly busy. (Not to mention the distraction of electronics.) But it can be done! This will take some planning but will be very rewarding.

How do you treat others? Is it your habit to respect and honor only certain people? God carefully formed each one making them very special to him. God personally gave you your family with the command for us to tend to their needs and wants. They should receive every kindness we can give them. People might forget what you do for them, but they never forget how you made them feel.

Romans 12:10...Be ye kindly affectioned one to another with brotherly love; in honour preferring one another:

I learned very early that I had to have a habit for cleaning my home. Dishes and laundry would have eaten me alive if I didn't! Right? Every morning while getting children dressed and rooms tidied, I did 2 loads of wash, piling the clothes on the couch to be folded during the school hours. After nap or quiet time, we had chore time. Chores were divided between children, with me assisting where needed. This schedule was kept every day, but Sunday, and it worked! I am here today because of that habit!

How about the habit of shopping and errands? With my busy homeschool family of 8, I learned to plan one day a week to be out in town. Piano lessons, library, lunch at the park and shopping, all in one. What is your habit? Try writing a shopping list and menu. Another great habit to have!

What about the habit of self-control? *one's ability to regulate one's emotions, thoughts, and behavior in the face of temptations.* This could be used in many areas of our life. Being responsible with our thought life, temper, eating, exercise, shopping, appearance, entertainment, work, bedtime...and I am sure there are more we could add. What area would the Lord want you to regulate?

What about those you spend time with? Do they draw you closer to the Lord and what he has for you or lead you away? There are lots of 'silly women' out there. They have little or no regard for the welfare of their family, home, or the things of God. If the Lord was coming to have lunch at your house would they be the guests that you would invite and want to introduce him too?

> *I Corinthians 15:33...Be not deceived: evil communications corrupt good manners.*
> *Proverbs 13:20...He that walketh with wise men shall be wise: but a companion of fools shall be destroyed.*

The things we do are our great defining markers. They are who we are. These habits define us and help us to use our time wisely, getting the most out of every minute. They are not always visible but are seen in our responses to what life throws our way. A 'glorious' daughter is very conscious of her habits and makes a point to develop good ones and to be faithful in them.

> **II Corinthians 5:17**...*Therefore if any man be in Christ, he is a new creature: old things are passed away; behold all things are become new.*

A little Homework...

1. What is one hypocritical habit that should not be in your life?

   a. What damage has it caused?

   b. What action can you take to make that habit disappear?

2. How many actions of anger do you exhibit in a day?
   *What can you do to stop that action?

3. Could you be classified as one of the 10 percent that do 90 percent of the work.

   * What can you do to be in that 10 percent?

4. Are you known for being prompt and on time, or late?
   * What 2 habits can you implement to be on time or have a better departure?

5. Does the look of your home say you are not lazy?
   * List 5 things to back up your answer.

6. What would bring about a negative spirit in your life?

   * What can you do to change that reaction.

7. Read Proverbs 31:10-31 and list 3 new habits that you can add to your life and how you plan to implement them.

Memory verse

Colossians 3:17...*And whatsoever ye do in word or deed, do all in the name of the Lord Jesus, giving thanks to God and the Father by him.*

Glorious in Her Habits

After-Action Report

I have been challenged in this area of our habits, how about you? We have learned that habits change things. For good or bad. We choose our habits, and in the end, they control the outcome of our lives. It is very important that you inventory your habits. Get rid of those that will bring about an unwanted end and invest in those, no matter how hard, that will bring about a 'Proverbs 31'and 'glorious daughter' end. In the long run it will be worth it all.

Here are a few examples of women having small habits that influenced the world.

> *Acts 16:13...And on the sabbath we went out of the city by a river side, where prayer was wont to be made; we sat down, and spake unto the women which resorted thither.*

The words, *where prayer was wont to be made*, is another way of saying, this is where the habit of praying was practiced. These ladies had a place, time and goal. It was no secret, and everybody knew who met there. Do you see that because of these ladies' open faithfulness, the gospel came to Philippi and many got saved? We don't know how long they kept this habit. We do know that God took notice and sent Paul and Silas. Their prayers brought about a vision that called Paul to come with the gospel! Don't give up on those good habits, dear 'glorious' daughters. Let them do their work. Realize that many habits take time to bear fruit.

> *I Samuel 2:19...Moreover his mother made him a little coat, and brought it to him from year to year, when she came up with her husband to offer the yearly sacrifice.*

Notice the habit this mother had for her son. She did not see him all year long, but she was foreseeing a need that he would have and planned to meet it. No one had to tell her that a coat would be needed. She could have said that the temple should provide the coat. After all, he worked there, far away from her. She had other children and demands to meet. Where would she find the time? You don't see the habit of selfishness or bitterness in her actions. I can't help but think that as she sewed that coat she prayed for God's blessings on his life. It was a habit she enjoyed. Are you investing in others faithfully? Those little unseen things many times hold everything together and show your real heart.

> *Luke 2:36,37...And there was one Anna, a prophetess, the daughter of Phanuel, of the tribe of Aser: she was of a great age, and had lived with an husband seven years from her virginity; And she was a widow of about fourscore and four years, which departed not from the temple, but served God with fastings and prayers night and day.*

What a picture of faithfulness! This woman sold out for the Lord. Notice that something happened to her husband after seven years of marriage and it doesn't list any children. It looks like some major sorrows were in her life. Where do we find her? Faithfully serving despite the circumstances. She continues a habit of sacrificial ministry to her Heavenly Father. We find her praying and fasting night and day. There are some habits that come to an end. Like raising children, or homeschooling, but we should always be investing in the Lord's ministry.

There is always something we could be doing. Even when we are in our latter years of life. What can you do for the Lord in your present circumstance?

These women each influenced the world with the habits in their lives. Paul received a vision to go to Philippi and a revival took place because Lydia and other women had a habit to pray. Hannah sacrificially met the needs of Samuel and he became the great priest of the Old Testament. And Anna served faithfully all the way through those latter years of life and saw the Messiah. Habits bring about a great return in the 'glorious' daughter's life. What fruit do you see in your future because of your habits?

> *I Chronicles 28:9...Know thou the God of thy father, and serve him with a perfect heart and with a willing mind: for the Lord searcheth all hearts, and understandeth all the imaginations of the thoughts: if thou seek him, he will be found of thee; but if thou forsake him, he will cast thee off for ever.*

You see everything goes back to our hearts and who we are trying to please. The 'glorious' daughter's top priority is the condition of her heart. Is she casting off those things that are displeasing and replacing them with godly things? Is she growing in the knowledge of the Lord? Ultimately her heart is making all her decisions for her. How she loves her husband, how she sacrifices for her heritage and chooses the habits she is going to exercise. The 'Glorious Daughter of the King' is very aware of these decisions and is constantly making sure they are pleasing to her heavenly Father.

A little Homework...

1. List 2 good habits you have implemented into your private thought life.

> * What benefits are you enjoying because of them?

2. List 2 negative habits of thinking that used to be in your life.

> * What blessings are you enjoying because of their absence?

3. List 2 good habits you have implemented into your public life.

> * What benefits are you enjoying because of them?

4. Write out Romans 12:2

   * List 3 things you can do to help you live this verse.

5. Write out II Corinthians 10:5.

   * What changes have you made to keep your thoughts under the obedience of Christ?

6. Are you current with your Bible reading schedule?

7. List the 5 negative public habits and their definitions.

   a. Which would be the most visible in your life?

   b. What 2 things can you do to change that?

8. If we were to describe your attitude as a piece of candy which one would you be?

* Skittles: colorful with variety
* Sweet Tarts: sweet and tangy
* Hot Tamales: Spicy and bold
* Sour Jellybeans: complaining and negative
* Jaw Breaker: unyielding and harsh

Memory Verse

***I Samuel 12:24**...Only fear the LORD, and serve Him in truth with all your heart: for consider how great things he hath done for you.*

Farewell

Dear 'glorious' daughter of the King.

I have so enjoyed this time with you. We have covered a lot of ground in these twenty-one lessons. I trust it has been as challenging and encouraging for you as it has been for me. Each lesson has had some trials and some rewards. But I think we all can agree that there is some work to be done and some great blessings to receive.

I hope that during the next few months you stay faithful and enjoy some great rewards for your efforts. There might be a few chapters you want to look back on to get some encouragement and direction as you continue growing into a "Glorious Daughter of the King." God bless you as you strive to bring Him glory and bear fruit that pleases Him.

Your Sister in Christ,

Debra Sommerdorf

About the Author

I was raised in a Christian home and saved at the age of seven through a *Good News Club* held in our home. At the age of fifteen I became awakened to spiritual things and surrendered my life to the Lord.

I married and joined my husband in Alaska in 1984. We assisted in planting and ministering in three churches, which included one on one discipleship in our home. During this time, we were blessed with six children...four girls and two boys.

My husband felt God leading him into evangelism and in the spring of 2000, we moved from a 1,900 square foot home to a 30-foot RV... totaling only 248 square feet. Thankfully home schooling was already a habit in our home, which helped tremendously in our adjustment to life on the road.

At this time five of our children are married, and we have eleven grandchildren, all of whom are being raised in the nurture and admonition of the Lord. Additionally, five of our six children are living for the Lord and faithfully serving Him through their local church.

Some of my hobbies include sewing, quilting, walking, reading, writing and visiting grandchildren. My life verse is found in, I Samuel 12:24..."*Only fear the LORD and serve him in truth with all your heart: for consider how great things he hath done for you.*" He has been so good to me!

Debra Sommerdorf

Phone: 800-231-0521
Email: info@48HrBooks.com
On-Line Chat: go to our website, www.48HrBooks.com